Steven Foster has one speed: Full-Throttle!

It's that commitment to going flat out that, in 2013, led him to embark on a thirty-four-day, thirty-four-state, 13,000-mile solo motorcycle ride along the perimeter of the United States wearing a pair of combat boots to raise awareness and support for the Boot Campaign, a national veterans service organization where he serves as an ambassador and advisory board member.

In *Full-Throttle Leadership: Passion, Power, & Purpose on the Edge of America,* Steven Foster recounts the most memorable places from "Sea to Shining Sea," but more importantly, the remarkable people who made his "Full-Throttle Leadership Ride" a life-changing experience.

Each mile riding alone through wicked thunderstorms, scorching heat, a mountain wildfire, and the constant deluge of assorted bugs, dirt, and grime—provides the backdrop for stories of the people he encountered in small towns and big cities across America who exemplified what is truly at the core of great leadership: service, sacrifice, and a commitment to helping others navigate the challenges of their own personal and professional "ride."

Their stories sustained him then and inspire him now as an advocate for giving back in the communities where we live, work, and meet; and it's that commitment that fuels his passion to inspire others to become "force multipliers for goodness."

You don't have to ride a motorcycle to become a full-throttle leader, but Steven's journey as a biker, entrepreneur, and Bucket Filler provides a road map for anyone on how to run wide open to serve the people who saddle up with you every day to do the work you do, whatever it may be.

If ever there was a moment to throttle up and refuel your own leadership ride, that moment is now.

. . . . . . . . . . . . . . . . . . . . . . . . . . . . . . . . . . . . . . . . . . . . . . . . . . . . . . . . . . . . . . . . . . . . . . . . . . . . . . .

Steven G. Foster, CMP is available for speaking engagements and book signings. To inquire about an appearance at your event, email to info@foster-fathom.com

Social Media Links:
www.linkedin.com/in/stevengfostercmp/
www.facebook.com/FosterandFathom
www.youtube.com/FosterFathom

Michael:
I met one of your
team members at MPI Houston
last week. She thought you
might enjoy the book.
All my best!!
/S

# FULL-THROTTLE LEADERSHIP

*Passion, Power, & Purpose on the Edge of America*

You didn't wake
up today to
be Mediocre.
Go Full-Throttle!
Steve Foster
8/3/22

## STEVEN G. FOSTER, CMP

Fulton Books
Meadville, PA

Published by Fulton Books 2021

Cover Photo Credit © Jakub Gojda

ISBN 978-1-64952-488-1 (paperback)
ISBN 978-1-63860-047-3 (hardcover)
ISBN 978-1-64952-489-8 (digital)

Printed in the United States of America

To the Original Boots Girls for showing us
that everyone can do something.

To Betty Garrett with Garrett Speakers International
for your friendship, support, and guidance throughout
this project. I wouldn't have made it without you.

To my mother, Carole Foster. Growing up, I didn't
fully see, understand, or even appreciate the sacrifices
you made for us as a single mom. I do now.

To my children, Aubrey and Conor; find something you care
about that makes the lives of others better and go *full throttle.*

To my wife, Wendy, everything good in
life begins and ends with you.

To the veterans, Gold Star Families, and active-duty
members of the US military, we owe you everything
and will never forget your service and sacrifice.

# CONTENTS

Biker Glossary ................................................................9

If I Have to Explain It, You Wouldn't Understand ........................11

Chapter 1:  Lone Survivor and Five "Boot Girls" from Texas .......15

Chapter 2:  The Capacity to Lead ............................................22

Chapter 3:  On the Road—the Gulf Coast (Kick Stands Up! [KSU]) ....................................................26

Chapter 4:  Passion—Find Your Ride ........................................34

Chapter 5:  Motorcycles and Team Success ...............................40

Chapter 6:  On the Road—the Atlantic Seaboard (KSU!) ..........48

Chapter 7:  Power—Fuel Your Ride ..........................................74

Chapter 8:  On the Road—the International Border (KSU!) .......81

Chapter 9:  Leaders, Check Your Mirrors! .................................92

Chapter 10: On the Road—the West Coast (KSU!) ....................98

Chapter 11: Purpose—Focus Your Ride ...................................109

Chapter 12: On the Road—Turning for Home (KSU!) .............115

Chapter 13: Wind Therapy ...................................................123

Chapter 14: Lessons Learned—The Ride Continues .................128

Afterword and Acknowledgements .........................................139

# BIKER GLOSSARY

AMA: American Motorcyclist Association

Cage/Cager: Motorcycle slang for a car and the driver

Chapter: The local entity of a larger club, i.e., Harley Owners Group, American Eagle Chapter

Cut: A leather or denim motorcycle vest

Farkle: Doodads, kitch, and add-ons that serve no useful purpose

Garage Rot: Motorcycles are meant to be ridden. If you leave your bike in the garage for too long, fluids dry up, parts deteriorate, and rust sets in. None of that is good.

HOG: Harley Owners Group

KSU: "Kick Stands Up." Everyone on the ride is "ready to roll."

OTB: Over the bars (crash). Never a good thing to do on a motorcycle.

Pin It: Run the speedometer needle as far as it will go.

Pod: A group of motorcycles traveling together in a supporting formation

Pucker Factor: A very close call when riding

Road Captain (RC): An experienced rider and chapter leader working as part of a team responsible for the planning, safety, and operation of a group ride

Rockers: Crescent-shaped patches sewn on a biker's cut that denote a team message, activity, or individual road name earned by participating in a chapter ride or activity

Twisties: A road with many curves, turns, and bends; very much sought after when riding a motorcycle

Waxer: A motorcycle owner who is more likely to spend time washing and waxing his bike than riding it. A poser.

# IF I HAVE TO EXPLAIN IT, YOU WOULDN'T UNDERSTAND

There is a popular saying in the motorcycle community: "If I have to explain *it*, you wouldn't understand."

For Bikers, **IT** is simply the deep appreciation for the freedom we feel when riding; a difficult connection to make with those who do not share the same experience. When riding, we instinctively understand the choices we make and the roads we take. And we are not focused solely on just destination but also, more importantly, who is along on the ride with us and why.

So perhaps you are wondering what riding motorcycles and leadership might possibly have in common. The image of a tattooed biker on a Harley-Davidson rolling down the highway while rocking out some Heavy Metal Thunder probably is not the first thing that comes to mind when conjuring up a leadership model. I appreciate your skepticism. A motorcycle makes for a cool visual, even an awesome team brand, but not where most organizations begin to look for leadership-development inspiration.

In the pages that follow, I hope to move your leadership GPS on the topic because after forty years riding motorcycles and more than twenty-five years working with some of the most successful leadership teams and professional organizations, what I know is this: whether you're tasked with managing a team to improve customer service, steering a department through a difficult transition, or working with other professionals to increase organizational value; when it comes to leadership, it's important you *know* **it** *and show* **it** and, critically, everyone involved *gets* **it***!*

Sadly, most organizations have no idea what **it** is.

The misconceptions of what make a great leader—individual stage presence, confidence, and vision—too often result in the wrong person being elevated into positions they simply aren't prepared for and clearly don't deserve. History is full of these examples: charismatic tyrants who ascended to power only to generate devastation and despair, arrogant warriors on a selfish quest for glory that resulted in epic massacres, and corporate wizards corrupted by greed and excess, bankrupting unsuspecting thousands.

What should be a clear leadership choice—getting a team of people focused on a common purpose, managing change, fueling success, and maintaining balance—often ends up in a heap of twisted perspectives and ruined expectation. Just as great leadership can power amazing accomplishments, failed leadership can wreck businesses, damage relationships, and tank reputations with devastating impact.

*Real* leadership success lives and lasts only when we inspire and encourage others on their personal and professional ride. I call this Full-Throttle Leadership, and it is the only fuel that powers sustainable team influence and success. In his book *Service*, author and former Navy SEAL Marcus Luttrell *(Lone Survivor)* writes this about serving others: "Service is selflessness—the opposite of the lifestyle that we see so much of in America today. The things that entertain us do not often lift us up or show us as the people we can rise to become."

Full-throttle leaders make us take notice. They change opinions, inspire actions, redirect thoughts, and alter outcomes.

I am often asked about the most memorable moments from my solo motorcycle ride around the perimeter of the country. There were many: the coastal views along the Overseas Highway to Key West, the raw emotion of the 9-11 Memorial in New York City, the power of Niagara Falls, the majestic Avenue of Giants in the Redwoods National Forest, the quirky artwork of the Enchanted Highway in Montana, and the vast landscape of the Algodones Dunes in California.

But what made the journey a life-changing experience were the remarkable people I met along the way. Two WWII veterans remembering acts of courage at Pearl Harbor and Normandy over a Sunday morning breakfast in New Orleans. A homeless Vietnam veteran in Norfolk who asked nothing for himself but hoped America would not abandon its returning Iraq and Afghanistan veterans. A young man in Billings, Montana, sharing the story of his brother, a decorated combat ranger who became one of the twenty-two veterans who commit suicide every day in our country. An Army dad at a roadside rest stop who wanted to give me gas money; his son was deployed overseas serving in harm's way.

I had the opportunity to see heroism, strength, service, and perseverance in people who, despite overwhelming odds, got up every day committed to making the lives of those around them better. Their stories sustained me across thirty-four days, thirty-four states, and 13,000 miles riding alone through wicked thunderstorms, scorching heat, a mountain wildfire, and the constant deluge of assorted bugs, dirt, and grime. Their influence made all the difference every day and in every way. And it continues.

You do not have to ride a motorcycle to be a full-throttle leader (it has, however, made my leadership journey a lot more fun!). What you absolutely must do is run wide open to serve the team—those people who saddle up every day to do the work you do, whatever it may be.

Leadership is service—plain and simple. It is "no limits, loud pipes, get your motor runnin', wind in your face blowin', free-bird playin', Heavy Metal Thunder screamin', born to be wild" full-throttle leadership!

If ever there was a moment to change your leadership focus, that moment is now.

It is time to transform your leadership efforts into what my friend, fellow biker, and Marine Corps veteran Jake Schick calls a "force multiplier for the greater good."

Let's roll! Let's ride!

CHAPTER 1

# LONE SURVIVOR AND FIVE "BOOT GIRLS" FROM TEXAS

*Full-Throttle Leadership* Road Rules:

> "The secret to fueling a satisfying life is realizing our unique opportunities to align passion, power, and purpose in service to others. Some people believe that is a hopelessly idealistic outlook. I'm not one of those people" (SGF).

Writing a book wasn't part of the plan when I began considering a motorcycle ride around the perimeter of the United States; neither was becoming a public advocate for active-duty servicemen and women, veterans, and military families. I was simply doing *me*, adding another experience to my Biker Bucket List; which, after forty years of riding, was already pretty full.

I've traveled some interesting roads on a motorcycle over the years, riding across the country to amazing places. I've been one of thousands of bikers from all over the world in Sturgis for the annual "world's largest" Motorcycle Rally and made the Four Corners run into the heart of the Navajo Nation with my riding buddy Bob Hicks where four states—Arizona, New Mexico, Utah, and Colorado—

intersect at one point on the map. One year, I rode to each of the Southeastern Conference (SEC) football stadiums during the off-season accompanied by veteran road warriors Glenn and Kim Christopher from the American Eagle HOG Chapter (Texas). We even managed to sneak our bikes into the team tunnels at several of them!

When you log more than 10,000 miles each year for more than a decade, you collect a lot of memories to go along with the T-shirts, rally pins, and rockers (those crescent-shaped patches on a biker's cut [vest] that say something about who you are, what you do, and how you do it out on the open road). Bikers have been sharing "viral" road stories through those rockers long before social media even existed.

The granddaddy of all rides, and one not many have the time or saddle strength to undertake, is along the US perimeter. The inspiration for this adventure was a fifty-three-year-old grandmother named Hazel Kolb, who, in 1979, jumped on her Harley-Davidson Electra Glide and rode around the United States—a journey which she chronicled in a book about the experience, *On the Perimeter.* Known as the "Motorcyclin' Grandma," she was a lifelong ambassador for the sport of motorcycling, becoming the first woman to serve on the American Motorcycle Association (AMA) Board of Trustees and was inducted into the association's Hall of Fame in 1998.

So in 2009, I began planning my own US-perimeter ride; and smack in the middle of researching destinations, mapping routes, scheduling stops, and booking hotels, it hits me: this is *big*! I'm about to go out on one of the great motorcycle adventures of all time. The entire Harley-Davidson community certainly will want to hear about it, and when it's done, I can look back at all I've accomplished and then wait for a phone call from the AMA Hall of Fame with my very own induction notice. Oh yeah!

Sounds like most of the so-called leadership we experience today, doesn't it? All about *me*!

An organizational team culture focused and fueled by individual expressions of *me, my,* and *I* is a surefire guarantee of trouble in the road ahead. It always leads to the same dead-end destination: burn-out, turnover, failure, and disconnect. No biker would ever consider spending time, talent, and treasure on a ride where just one person made all the decisions about where to go, how to get there, and what to do based solely on that individual's need and exclusive benefit.

And yet we continue to accept this tired and flawed approach to leadership in almost every area of our lives that matters personally and professionally.

There is no *leadership* or *development* in an endeavor that doesn't inspire, engage, and make an impact beyond individual gain or some itemized set of organizational goals. On the road to team success, you must ask yourself some important questions before setting out together:

- Where are you going?

- Who is riding with you?

- How will you get there?

- What keeps you rolling?

- Why does it matter?

By early 2009, I was well into planning my perimeter ride, so I already knew the answers to the first three questions and had some ideas on the fourth. But the most important answer for any leader or team member to ask—*why*—was a bit vague. I knew it would be great fun and personally rewarding, no doubt. There would certainly be many photos ops at memorable sites to share on my social-media sites and some interesting stories on my return home, so it had all the makings of an extraordinary trip.

But then what?

If I was going to commit significant time, expense, and effort, the ride should be something more than just "one man on one motorcycle" riding around the country with no purpose other than just to say he did it. What I needed was a reason to ride beyond just me. I didn't have one, so my excellent adventure on the edge of America kept being postponed year after year.

Then a book and a pair of combat boots changed everything.

The book—*Lone Survivor: The Eyewitness Account of Operation Redwing and the Lost Heroes of SEAL Team 10* by Marcus Luttrell— was recommended to me by a friend. It's a powerful story of service, sacrifice, courage, and heroism told by the only survivor of an extraordinary firefight in Afghanistan that led to the largest loss of life in US Navy SEAL history since World War II.[1]

In June 2005, a four-man SEAL team went deep behind enemy lines to conduct a reconnaissance mission to locate a high-ranking Taliban leader. The SEALs, Lt. Michael Murphy, Gunner's Mate 2nd Class Danny Dietz, Sonar Technician 2nd Class Matthew Axelson, and Luttrell, a hospital corpsman 2nd class, were discovered by local tribesman who reported their location to Taliban insurgents.

---

[1] On August 6, 2011, a CH-47 Chinook helicopter (call sign Extortion 17) was shot down in the Wardak province, killing all thirty-eight people on board— twenty-five American special-operations personnel, five United States Army National Guard and Army Reserve crewmen, seven Afghan commandos, and one Afghan interpreter—as well as a US military working dog. The deaths surpassed Operation Red Wings as the worst loss of American lives in a single incident in the Afghanistan campaign.

Their mission compromised, outnumbered, and overwhelmed, the SEALs fought back against the enemy through the mountains of the Hindu Kush while waiting for rescue. An MH-47 Chinook helicopter with a Quick Reaction Force of Navy SEALs and army Night Stalkers raced to the rescue, but a rocket-propelled grenade struck the helicopter, killing all sixteen men aboard.

On the ground and nearly out of ammunition, the four SEALs continued to fight. Murphy, Axelson, and Dietz were eventually killed in action. Luttrell, severely wounded, evaded the enemy and was protected by Pashtun villagers who risked their lives to keep him safe from pursuing Taliban fighters. One of the villagers walked to a marine outpost with a note from Luttrell, and US forces rescued him four days later.

*Lone Survivor* is an absolute must-read for any leader. It's not just an epic combat story (although it certainly is that) but also a powerful lesson in service, sacrifice, and commitment to team. It had an immediate impact on everyone who read it, including five women from Texas who immediately began looking for a way to actively support our troops beyond just flying a flag or putting a yellow ribbon sticker on a vehicle. But how and where to start?

Sherri Reuland, Leigh Ann Ranslem, Ginger Giles, Heather Sholl, and Mariae Bui were inspired to do something and came up with a remarkable idea that—unknown to them at the time—would eventually provide a lasting opportunity for Americans to express their patriotism while providing meaningful support to active-duty servicemen and women, veterans, and military families. Their idea was based on an adage as old as time itself: "You'll never understand or appreciate someone until you walk in their shoes."

Or in this case, *boots.*

Fueled with a passion to serve and several pairs of combat boots purchased from a local Army Navy store, the five friends, now affectionately known as the Original Boot Girls, set out to help promote a military-benefit concert with a unique photo op: getting people to pose for pictures in combat boots and making a donation to a local veterans event. Their idea connected in a big way; and soon they began hearing from others who wanted to help, among them former Texas governor Rick Perry, radio/TV host Glenn Beck, and countless Americans who were inspired by the idea of wearing combat boots as a show of personal support and gratitude for our troops. With the lace of a boot, a movement was born.

The Boot Campaign (www.bootcampaign.com) is a powerful example of what anthropologist and activist Margaret Mead was referring to when she said, "Never doubt that a small group of thoughtful, committed citizens can change the world; indeed, it's the only thing that ever has." No one, not even the Boot Girls, could have imagined the trail they were about to blaze in the veteran-service nonprofit world with that first small photo op in a pair of used combat boots.

Since its inception in 2011, the Boot Campaign has raised more than twenty million dollars, giving more than two million dollars annually to help service members, veterans, and their families from every generation. With a vision to promote patriotism, raise awareness of the unique challenges service members face during service and post-service, and provide assistance to military personnel, past and present, and their families; the Boot Campaign has funded post-traumatic stress (PTS) counseling services, family therapy, prosthetics and mobility equipment, wellness retreats for military couples, and mortgage-free home grants, just to name a few.

In 2016, the Boot Campaign initiated a Health and Wellness Program led by former Navy SEAL and cognitive neuroscientist Morgan Luttrell (Marcus' twin brother) focused on providing veterans access to world-class physical and mental wellness programs for traumatic brain injury (TBI), post-traumatic stress disorder (PTSD), chronic pain, addiction, and insomnia. By removing financial barriers, the Boot Campaign ensures our servicemen and women can receive the treatment that they deserve and have earned. Its ground-breaking stuff, and it works.

No single organization has the ability to solve the diverse and complex challenges that face our military community, so today Boot Campaign has joined joins forces with like-minded entities to steward veterans and their families through life-changing treatment and training to *reclaim* health and wellness, *restore* families, *restart* careers, *reduce* suicide, and *reinforce* communities.

When you give back to help others, your actions and words become greater, more powerful, and sustainable. That's leadership defined.

A Navy SEAL and five women inspired me to transform my personal bucket-list item into a cause: *the Full-Throttle Leadership Ride*—a thirty-four-day, thirty-four-state, 13,000-mile solo adventure along the US perimeter to raise awareness and support for the Boot Campaign. I set up a fundraising page and dedicated each day of the ride to an active-duty service member or veteran. I accepted a much bigger challenge than just riding around America on a motorcycle; my goal now was to influence everyone I met along the way to live out the Boot Campaign's mission: "When they come back, we give back."

We don't always know where our choices will take us. I certainly couldn't see the full impact of what I was about to do or that a simple change in outlook was about to lead me to people and places that forever changed my outlook and outcome both personally and professionally.

CHAPTER 2

# THE CAPACITY TO LEAD

*Full-Throttle Leadership* Road Rules:

> Just because you're going flat out doesn't mean
> you're on the right road!

Leadership sits atop every "must have" list for any individual and organization seeking lasting success. Type *leadership* into a Google Search, and you get an astonishing 2.1 billion matches. Add the keyword *theories* to your leadership search, and the hits reveal an additional 128 million possibilities.

Maybe you've experienced a few of them. It's a good bet you have watched a video on leadership, attended a leadership conference or a training session on leadership, or sat through a leadership lecture. There are leadership academies, labs, networks, summits, groups, links, forums, institutes, and centers. And despite all those leadership opportunities, organizations and individuals are still endlessly hungry for information on the subject.

It seems like we've logged many miles on the search for great leadership but haven't made much progress on the journey.

It's not because we don't have enough information on the subject. The leadership road is cluttered with popular (and competing) concepts and theories, among them power leadership, authentic leadership, organizational leadership, networked leadership, and ecological leadership, just to name a few. One popular methodology emerged a few years ago applying numbers, colors, and animals to identify an individual leadership style—as if classifying yourself as a "Number 2, Green; Gorilla" would compel anyone to follow your lead.

What makes leadership success so elusive isn't the abstract; it's the application. According to the *Merriam-Webster Dictionary, leadership* is defined as "the capacity to lead."

If you're surprised by that description, perhaps it's because we've so diluted the meaning of leadership ever since the first research on the subject took place at the start of the nineteenth century. At that time, it was determined there simply was no single characteristic or combination of traits that clearly explained this elusive ability.

Leadership research pioneer R. M. Stogdill took a run at the subject in 1974 when he authored the *Handbook of Leadership: a Survey of Theory.* His examination identified six characteristics associated with leadership, but he noted, "No one becomes a leader simply by possessing a certain list of character traits." During the 1980s, *situational leadership* became the key area of focus, and it was determined people were capable of being a follower or a leader depending upon the situation they were placed into.

Finally, research in the 1990s and early 2000s concluded that all previous leadership research was insufficient because it relied on outdated leadership models. A frustrating return to square one.

Truthfully, there are miles between what we say we *know* about leadership and what we actually *do* as leaders. If you want to be a successful leader, start by discovering your capacity to lead—your it—and using *it* to influence, impact, and inspire others to the best of your abilities. Everyone's **it** will be different (stylistically), but engaging **it** in service to others will undeniably fuel the distinguishing difference you want to make as a leader.

Author Simon Sinek has written of the importance of identifying leadership capacity as a road map to identifying the contribution and impact you want to make in the world personally and professionally in his book, *Start with Why.* Discovering what you're capable of accomplishing—doing what you can do *right now*—helps move you move beyond the usual and routine toward a destination where you can be more, do more, and become more than you ever thought possible.

So let's revisit that simple dictionary definition.

If we're all *capable* of leadership, and I believe that to be true, then finding the best focus and fuel for our leadership efforts becomes much more important to success than style (characteristics) or fashion (situation). Look at it this way. I know many people who own Harley-Davidson T-shirts but have never ridden a motorcycle. That's okay. You do *you.*

The Latin root word for *authentic* is *author.* And since we're focusing on definitions, an author is "one that originates or creates; a source." There's even an **it** in *authenticity.* Authentic leadership then is an active and adaptable process. It's about building your unique capability to influence others.

That's exactly how my perimeter ride began, a journey on motorcycles with some friends that would result in great memories and experiences while checking off big-trip items on my personal Biker Bucket List. And that would have been enough, or so I thought at the time. Fortunately, circumstances intervened. The closer the departure date, my fellow riders began to drop out, and what started as a group ride quickly was paired down to just me. At that point, I had to ask myself: without anyone along to share the memories and experiences, *why* would *it* matter, beyond just my singular accomplishment? And the answer was, I really didn't know.

Fortunately, I found the Boot Campaign, and its mission to "create awareness, promote patriotism, and provide assistance" was just the fuel I needed to do what I could do—ride a motorcycle— and engage others along the way. Riding for *them* took the focus off me, something all leaders should strive for. It unleashed my capacity to make a difference and opened me up to discovering some powerful moments along every mile of the journey.

One such example arrived in the form of a small crystal ornament just weeks before I was set to depart.

My friend Alison Kieckhafer, CMP, was serving as president of the Meeting Professionals International Dallas/Fort Worth Chapter and had chosen a powerful theme for her leadership term: "Activate Your Goodness." She challenged all 800-plus chapter members to act on improving the community and the larger world around them with a simple message: "Think good, speak good, and do good."

She was onto something *big*!

Much like a military challenge coin, which bears a unit or branch insignia and is carried by its members to signify camaraderie, Alison presented each chapter member with her ornament and urged them to find a charitable organization and work on its behalf during the year. I had the Boot Campaign, so I hitched her Goodness Crystal to the saddlebag of my Harley-Davidson as an ever-present reminder I was riding for a cause, not applause.

Plans made, route set, and destinations confirmed. Time to hit the road and get to work.

CHAPTER 3

# ON THE ROAD—THE GULF COAST (KICK STANDS UP! [KSU])

*Full-Throttle Leadership* Rules of the Road:

> "I don't really feel like going for a ride today," said no biker ever!

On each day of the ride, I posted my experiences online in the Full-Throttle Leadership Ride blog. Excerpts appear in some of the following chapters, but you can follow the full journey with photos at http://www.foster-fathom.com/road-stories.

From the Full-Throttle Leadership Ride (FTLR) Blog

Dallas, Texas, to Key West, Florida—2,251.5 miles

Friday, June 28, 2013

Day 1: Dallas, TX, to Houston, TX—377.50 Miles

I'm headed south to Houston, ready for whatever is waiting for me along the way. Wouldn't you know it; the first leadership lesson arrives unexpectedly before I roll out of the driveway.

I put my shoes on every day as I head out the door and never give it a second thought. You probably don't either. This morning, however, I am lacing up a pair of the Boot Campaign's signature military combat boots, the same ones I will wear each day on every mile of The Full-Throttle Leadership Ride. Unlike slipping into my regular shoes, it takes a bit more focus and effort to lace up a pair of combat boots. You can't do it casually.

How blessed we are to have men and women willing to put their "boots on the ground" to keep our nation free, safe, and strong. That's the essence of leadership: selfless, focused, and ready to roll in service to others. I say a quick prayer for the amazing adventure ahead and to be reminded every day of those who serve and safeguard the many freedoms we enjoy as Americans.

I think of family members who served: my father (Air Force), my Uncle Al (Navy), and older brother Major Rod. W Cromer, a career Army officer. Even my Grandfather, who was medically disqualified from service (although he tried several times), found a way to assist the U.S.

Coast Guard by captaining a patrol boat along the Alabama Gulf Coast during WWII.[2]

Despite being born into a military family on an Air Force base in California, no one was surprised when I chose a different career; first as a journalist, and now a speaker and author. Those experiences served me well for the journey I'm about to begin as an advocate for veterans and military families; could it be karma or coincidence aligning to bring life full circle?

Today is dedicated to the memory of Gary Truitt (08/07/1947–04/31/2011), Special Services, former police officer, motorcyclist, and Mason. Gary's best friend Michael Collins made a special donation through the FTLR CrowdRise Page in his honor.

Day 2: Saturday, June 29, 2013/Houston to New Orleans—475 Miles

It's Boots on the Bayou as The Full-Throttle Leadership Ride (FTLR) rolls into The Big Easy. New Orleans is absolutely one of my favorite places anywhere in the world. My nephew, David Cromer, left Houston with me this morning, so I had an official "Support Vehicle" on Day 2 of FTLR.

---

[2] My grandfather, Ernest M. Foster, used to tell us stories of how he patrolled the Gulf Coast during WWII looking for German submarines. Of course, we laughed. Everyone knew WWII water battles were fought in the Atlantic and Pacific Oceans. Then in 2014, scientists discovered the sunken U-boat 166, which torpedoed and sank the SS *Robert E. Lee* off the coast of Mississippi on July 30, 1942. This is just a few miles from where my grandfather patrolled!

It's HOT in the Deep South, and I expect that to continue as I wind my way through Alabama and Florida over the next week. Tomorrow morning's Ride starts with something special. Stay Tuned!

Today's Ride is dedicated to my brother and David's dad, Major Rod. W. Cromer, U.S. Army (Retired). Rod knew he wanted to be a soldier since he was a boy, and he certainly achieved his dream, serving in Louisiana, Texas, Hawaii, and finally at The Pentagon. Later, he mentored young people in a high school ROTC Program in Alabama. I salute you, brother!

Day 3: Sunday, June 30, 2013/New Orleans, LA, to Panama City Beach, FL—410 miles

The morning began with a special reminder of just what this Ride is all about.

Clem Goldberger with the National WWII Museum in New Orleans arranged a special interview with two WWII veterans, Bert Stolier and Tom Blakey. If you're not familiar with the National WWII Museum, you absolutely must plan a visit there. It opened on June 6, 2000, and was founded by historian and author Stephen Ambrose. The Museum showcases the American Experience throughout WWII—why it was fought, how it was won, and what it means today.

Both men were straightforward and humble when discussing their military service, refusing to be called what broadcaster Tom Brokaw termed

"The Greatest Generation," but I think description is most appropriate and well-deserved. Throughout our interview, Bert and Tom shared lessons learned as young men growing up in a World at War. They candidly discussed their own personal struggles after returning home from military service, raising families, building businesses, and sadly, living in a country, both said, at times they hardly recognize as Home.

It was an honor to spend Sunday morning with Bert and Tom. They are REAL American Heroes.

I am SERIOUSLY PUMPED UP leaving New Orleans. Heading east along I-10 and eventually to US Highways 90, 98, 41, and 1 crossing through four states—Louisiana, Mississippi, Alabama, and Florida. In Mississippi, I run alongside some colorful pre-World War II vintage automobiles competing in the 2013 Hemmings Motor News Great Race. This year's race from St. Paul, MN, to Mobile, AL, covered 10 States in 9 Days for 2,100 miles. It was great to see so many other people out on the road enjoying a trek across America, and the vintage cars remind me of my time with Bert and Tom. Lunch with my brother, Rod; his wife Joyce in Mobile, where I also say goodbye to my temporary support vehicle driver, my nephew David. From here on, I ride solo. The sun sets as I leave my hometown, Mobile, Alabama, and head off along the Gulf Coast. Next stop, Panama City.

Day 4: July 1, 2013/Panama City Beach, FL, to
Fort Myers, FL—607 Miles

Rolled out in the Florida sunshine, headed
down the 98 Coastal Highway. Began the morning saluting the men and women of the US Air
Force at Tyndall AFB, home of the 325th Fighter
Wing (Air Dominance).

Then it was off on some of the best beach riding anywhere: Mexico Beach, Apalachicola, and
Carrabelle (home to the world's smallest police
station and birthplace of "Buck" O'Neil, legendary Negro American League player and manager).
Nothing like riding in the Florida sunshine!

And then the skies opened, and as Mother
Nature showed, her rains came.

Blinding, wind-whipped thunderstorms,
and ground-striking lightning were my scary
companions for the final 300 miles through
Chiefland, St. Petersburg, Bradenton, Sarasota,
and Port Charlotte into Fort Myers. What was
supposed to be an 8-hour scenic ride along
Florida beaches flooded away to become a miserable, bone-chilling 14-hour dash for cover. Rain
poured its way through every layer of protective
gear I had available. At each stop—and there were
many—I questioned the sanity and safety of slog-
ging along—cold, wet, miserable, and alone—in
seriously dangerous thunderstorms. There weren't
many places I could simply pull in and rest; so
I took the few abandoned gas stations or closed
roadside produce stands that were available to me
and waited for the storms to pass. They never did.

The rest of the day was filled with short sprints, frequent stops, and the occasional convenience-store coffee to warm me up. I arrived drained and drenched, with water jetting up and out of the tops of my boots when I set the kickstand down and emptying rain out of my helmet like a waterfall.

Hot shower, food, and bed...here I come!

Day 5: Tuesday, July 2, 2013/No GO!

I'm scheduled to ride on to Key West, but at 6:00 am this morning, still more lightning and thunderstorms outside. It's cold, wet, and coming down in buckets, so I'm obviously not going anywhere today but to the hotel laundromat. I lay there in my dark room feeling not so lucky anymore.

Later in the day did a Skype interview with Jeff Brady, host of The Texas Daily on KTXD-TV in Dallas. Thanks to the fabulous Betty Garrett with Garrett Speakers International for arranging this. The interview airs in Dallas on the 4th of July. Back on the bike tomorrow, hopefully, as the FTLR heads to Key West!

Day 6: Wednesday, July 3, 2013/Fort Myers, FL, to Key West, FL—382 Miles

After a full day of rest and drying out from the thunderstorms, or so I thought, it was an early morning KSU to Key West. Rolled down

US 41, The Tamiami Trail, also known as Alligator Alley, through the Heart of the Florida Everglades. Amazing, scenic, somewhat scary ride—they don't call it Alligator Alley for nothing. The gators DO cross the road!

Something darted out in front of me on a long, narrow stretch of rainy Everglades Road. It was big, fast, and black; not sure if it was a Skunk Ape (Florida's Bigfoot), Gator Man, or some Alien from the Bermuda Triangle, but it made for an exciting start to the Ride.

U.S. 1 North passes through Islamorada, Key Largo, Ramrod Key, Annie's Beach, Marathon, Duck Key—and words don't do the view justice. Some of the most beautiful green water you will ever see. I wondered how much greener and more beautiful it would be without more pop-up thunderstorms interrupting the ride?

Finally made it to Key West. Headed down to Duval Street. Lunch at the Hogs Breath Saloon and then took in the sights and sounds. No wonder everyone from John Audubon, Ernest Hemingway, Thomas Edison, Lou Gehrig, Harry Truman, and Tennessee Williams all spent time here.

Week One and Done!

Daily rides this week were in honor of Bert, Tom, and the all the WWII veterans who volunteer at the National WWII Museum; and Bill Copeland, USAF, his sons Allen and Josh, who are both currently serving in the army; and to all those serving at Naval Air Station (NAS) in Key West.

CHAPTER 4

# PASSION—FIND YOUR RIDE

Full-Throttle Leadership Road Rules:

> Position doesn't make you a leader. Action makes
> you a leader.

It's been said there are "three ways to develop great leadership, but no one knows what they are."

WWII veterans Bert Stolier and Tom Blakey were the exceptions to the rule.

On a bright Sunday morning at the National WWII Museum[3]* in New Orleans, these WWII veterans recalled moments and memories from their incredible lives. Bert, who was ninety-four years old at the time and ran three miles every day, enlisted in the Marines in 1940 and served throughout the Pacific. He was stationed at Pearl

---

[3]   Any organization or individual genuinely interested in learning about leadership should invite a WWII veteran to lunch or to speak to your team. According to recent statistics from the Veterans Administration, their numbers are below 1 million, a small fraction of the 16 million Americans who served during WWII. We are losing these men and women and their memories at a rate of 492 each day. Their experiences and insights into leadership service and sacrifice are invaluable, a national treasure, which will be gone too soon.

Harbor during the Japanese attack on Dec. 7, 1941, and later was assigned to the USS *Northampton*, which was torpedoed and sunk off Guadalcanal at night during the Battle of Tassafaronga. Tom, ninety-three, enlisted in the army, graduated from jump school, and joined the 82nd Airborne Division. He parachuted into Normandy on D-Day, June 6, 1944, and later saw action at the Battle of the Bulge.

Their wisdom, life lessons, leadership service, and personal sacrifice provided clear-cut examples of the singularly essential quality every great leader must possess and, more importantly, be able to inspire in others: *passion.*

I define *passion* as a strong conviction or loyalty, a purposeful interest in an idea or activity resulting in good work done on behalf of others rather than an obsessive desire for something, usually for ourselves. When it comes to leadership, that's a difference worth noting.

"When you lead men, you do it with the thought of what's not just good for you but always what's best for them," Bert said.

Tom recalled his commanding officer, Lt. General James Maurice Gavin, who earned the nickname "Jumpin' Jim" because of his practice of taking part in combat jumps with the paratroopers under his command. Gavin, the only American general officer to make four combat jumps during WWII, was a West Point graduate who also fought against segregation in the US Army. He earned the respect of his men because, as Tom said, "he loved us enough to get down in the mud and dirt with us."

"Gavin could take the entire 505 [505th Parachute Infantry Regiment], put them toe to toe at the edge of the Grand Canyon, and say 'jump,' and every one of us would have jumped because he would have jumped first," he said with a smile.

Bert agreed. "Our leaders believed they could handle anything, and they made us believe we could too," then adding, "We were told we had a job to do. That was it. We did it, and thank God, we came home."

One of my favorite leadership quotes is "A leader is a dealer in hope."

It's a curious perspective on leadership, especially in light who said it and what it reveals about the nature of authentic leadership; in this case, the eighteenth-century emperor of France, Napoleon Bonaparte, not someone often quoted as a symbol of inspiration and hope.

Napoleon was a great military commander but also a brutal dictator. He waged relentless wars and conquered most of the known European powers of his day. In his lust for power and authority, 500,000 of his army lay dead in the snow outside Moscow, and eventually he suffered an overwhelming defeat at Waterloo that ended in exile. Maybe I need to get a new favorite leadership quote.

Or maybe, as leaders, we need to care about our people and not just our own authority. Authentic leadership keeps everyone inspired, involved, and moving forward together. It separates the intentional from the accidental.

A leader who deals *hope* creates passion for the possible. Passion lies in your singular capability to influence and engage others with conviction and authenticity, the first and most important roll on the leadership throttle. Passion, therefore, becomes an exercise in identifying the two of the most important steps on any journey:

- Where are you going?

- Who is riding with you?

When you know where you're going and who is riding with you, your capacity to accomplish and become successful improves exponentially. Endless possibilities open when you roll on that throttle. When passion guides the ride, everyone involved *gets it.*

Bert and Tom told me that riding my motorcycle around the country was (literally and figuratively) the "vehicle" that would get me *where* I wanted to go, but serving others was what would make the journey successful. I knew then the ride wasn't about me or a bucket list. I was riding *for* Bert and Tom and people I had yet to meet who needed me to use my passion for riding to share their stories, to say thank you, and perhaps to bring some attention and support to a cause bigger than a guy from Texas on a motorcycle ride around the country.

Throughout our conversation, Bert and Tom were genuine and humble when discussing their military service. I was grateful to share some time with these remarkable men and told them so.

"Everyone is lucky sometimes," Bert said with a sly grin, recalling his combat experiences in the Pacific Theater during WWII. "It's what you do with luck that matters."

Bert Stolier returned to New Orleans after the war and, with his wife Marian, owned and operated a string of Swenson's ice-cream parlors. When the National World War II Museum opened, Bert quickly became one of seven WWII-veteran volunteers known as the "A-Team" who shared war-time experiences with thousands of visitors. He was awarded the Museum's Silver Service Medallion in 2015 in recognition of his service in the Marine Corps and in retirement. He also was honored with a dedicated seat in the museum's Solomon Victory Theater and a commemorative brick in the Campaigns of Courage Pavilion.

Bert Stolier died on June 13, 2016. He was ninety-seven years old and the longest-serving WWII-veteran museum volunteer.

Tom Blakey relocated to New Orleans after the war and founded Blakey's Log Service, an oil field supply company. He was called the museum's "Number One Volunteer," contributing 15,000 volunteer hours as a speaker and interpretive guide. One of his favorite stories was how a child's toy, known as the "cricket," played a vital role in the D-Day invasion. US troops would click the noisemaker, which "chirped" like the insect it was named for whenever they contacted unidentified troops. Tom said if you received a click back with the correct coded response, "you knew you had a friend."

More than 160,000 Allied troops landed along a fifty-mile stretch of heavily fortified coastline on the beaches of Normandy, France, with 5,000 ships and 13,000 aircraft supporting the D-Day invasion in its battle with Nazi Germany. By day's end, more than 9,000 Allied soldiers were killed or wounded.

Blakey, who was a recipient of the French Legion of Honor Medal, returned to Normandy eight times after the war, including during the seventieth anniversary of D-Day in 2014. Toward the end of his life, Tom revealed he had suffered severely from the effects of PTSD for nearly seventy years. It affected his personal relationships for decades, and he hoped by speaking out, he could help those young men and women similarly returning home from Iraq and Afghanistan who were affected.

Tom Blakey died in his home on January 15, 2015. He was ninety-four years old. Hundreds attended his memorial service in the US Freedom Pavilion at the National World War II Museum.

Bert and Tom, like so many of the "greatest generation," were national treasures. They understood passion can be your GPS to find a meaningful *route to stand out* as a person and a professional. Passion reminds us to slow down and that riding faster than everyone else only guarantees you'll ride alone.

A leader who deals hope creates passion for the possible. That's a ride everyone wants to join.

Find your passion. Find your ride.

CHAPTER 5

# MOTORCYCLES AND TEAM SUCCESS

Full-Throttle Leadership Road Rules:

> "Motorcycles tell us a powerful leadership truth: we are small and exposed and probably moving too fast for our own good" (Zen and the Art of Motorcycle Maintenance: an Inquiry into Values by Robert Pirsig).

Organizations do some strange things in the name of leadership and team development.

Some believe it's the "name over the door," and if everyone will just "logo up," the team will somehow be magically "branded" into existence. Team character, loyalty, or success aren't created with bad corporate fashion. Others are "stuck" doing what's comfortable and familiar, riding along in the same direction at the same speed with the same predetermined priorities and conclusions and expecting a different result. These organizations never commit the time to fully identify what matters most to increase effectiveness or improve the environment necessary for a team to get where they need to go right from the start.

Developing a group of diverse individuals into a team that can move together successfully, without incident, toward a predetermined destination doesn't happen by accident. Success demands outfitting every person for their unique place in the pod if you expect to be *ready to roll* when it's time to go kick stands up! It requires time, training, and attention to detail. That's why they call it leadership *development*. What wrecks a successful team ride is poor preparation, skewed skill sets, and false assumptions; and no T-shirt or name badge can compensate for that.

If we were meeting today at my home in Dallas to ride down to the Texas Hill Country (a three-hour ride with some of the most picturesque views in the state) and half of us showed up on Harleys and the other half arrived on mopeds; we would be going nowhere fast. Both have similar features (two wheels, handlebars, seat, and throttle), but that's where the comparisons end. No self-respecting biker is going to accept the limitations of motoring along at 31 miles per hour across 212 miles on an eight-hour caravan crawl, stopping every 75 miles for fuel to accommodate the smaller machines.

Setting off with people ill-equipped to start and finish *together* is a ride destined to fail.

Remember that leadership **it**?

Most organizations fail because they would rather defend what they've always done rather than doing something about it, whatever *it* may be. They make excuses and waste time overthinking, rehashing, grumbling, and whining about whatever *it* is. And just like a motorcycle, *it* isn't going anywhere unless you get the right fuel in the tank.

Leadership, like a fuel injector, is an important but often volatile delivery system. Both exist to optimize power, efficiency, performance reliability, and range. But introduce something (or someone) detrimental into the mix, and nothing performs the way it's supposed to. How many of us have worked somewhere where everyone was pushed to exceed goals and give more but there was little or nothing new in the way of resources, inspiration, and support to accomplish the mission?

If your team isn't making any real progress, check the leadership tank.

People working on endless demand, insufficient gratitude, and mounting pressure eventually run dry and burn out. That's when full-throttle leaders are needed most. They listen, teach, encourage, and help others get where they want to go. Full-throttle leaders changes opinions, inspires actions, redirects thoughts, and alters outcomes. They make the journey meaningful for the people who *ride* with them.

I've experienced this working with the Road Captain (RC) Team at the American Eagle Harley Owners Group (HOG) in Texas. These experienced riders—all volunteers—interact with members in a variety of ways: attending chapter meetings and events, encouraging chapter involvement, and leading training sessions where participants can learn bike control and group-riding tactics. The RCs schedule rides, research destinations, and plan events while, at the same time, constantly improving their own advanced road skills— which includes completing an Experienced Rider Course every few years.

On the group ride, RCs communicate with members in their pod (team) through a precise method of predetermined hand signals, everything from pointing (with hand or foot) to identifying hazards in the roadway. Each signal is designed to nonverbally convey safety or ride information throughout the pod. It's a leadership language vital to the ride's success.

Serving as a road captain also offers a unique opportunity to receive individual feedback from members who can present RCs with *rockers* (the biker version of a name tag) marking memorable individual moments, experiences, or encounters on their journeys together. Presenting a rocker is a very personal way of commemorating the journey. It also serves to recognize those who led or contributed to the shared experience by marking an occasion or memorable occurrence.

It's true; what happens on the road—the good, bad, fun, and foolish—**never** stays on the road (or around the leadership table either for that matter!).

Some of my favorite rockers belong to RCs who are not just expert riders but also are good leaders on and off the bike. They include the following:

- Paul "Whiff" Martin

  Earned while attempting to ring the bell on a carnival high striker game. Paul made a very large swing with an even bigger hammer, completely missing the strike pad in full view of everyone. Immediately, he heard someone shout, "That's a whiff." Paul served as director of the chapter and was one of the most experienced riders I ever saw, cool under pressure and a solid leader.

- David "Captain Marvel" Barnes

  Earned for putting together a weekend ride on the fly. Everyone *marveled* at David's skill at navigation and uncanny ability to find great roads to ride. One member said, "I bet Captain Marvel will find us a fun road." David, another chapter director, is always ready to ride. Trusted by everyone, he always finds a way to make the ride fun.

- Doug "Mini T" Hull

    Earned when a member, who didn't know his name, commented, "You look like a mini version of Tony" (the chapter director at the time). To avoid confusion, he was given the rocker "Mini-T." It stuck. To this day, many members still don't even know his real name is Doug. At first glance, most people see Doug as an imposing figure— he's a big guy—but he has an even bigger heart. He's the ultimate wingman and road brother.

- Scotty *"Sippy Kup"* Brauer

    Earned when he spilled a large glass of tea during a dinner ride. One of those who was splashed asked *"what do we have to do, get you a Sippy-Kup?"* Scotty is the most fun person to be around, quick with a great story and an even better laugh. He's the real "Fun Boss."

- Bert "Left Side" Williams

    Earned during a refueling stop after a long day riding in the rain. Tired and soaked, Bert pulled up to a gas pump and started to set his bike down, leaning to the right. Unfortunately, the kickstand is on the left side of the bike. He realized his mistake as soon as the heavily loaded bike started to go over. Lesson learned, Left Side! Bert is solid and steady. Nothing ever seems to rattle him. He inspires confidence.

- Jim "Harley Stew" Klinect

    I presented this rocker to Jim, our head road captain at the time, and several other members of the RC team during a HOG Cruise in 2014. Prior to leaving for an excursion in Cozumel, several of the guys decided to skip breakfast and take a soak in the ship's hot tub. Someone snapped a photo of us and with bubbles and steam rising. We looked like we were cooking in a big stew pot. Jim rides with his entire family, and that's how he treats everyone. Just a good dude.

The rockers stuck. Some were funny, some celebrated misadventures, but each one became a permanent identifier of membership in our biker tribe. They were warmly received and proudly worn as a badge of service and support by leaders who made our rides together memorable, safe, and successful.

Don't ever underestimate the importance of the people you *ride* with every day. They know you perhaps better than most because they share the journey. Your *road stories* either connect everyone involved in a powerful and positive way or completely wreck organizations and reputations often beyond repair.

How proudly would your organization's leaders wear a *rocker* based on the personal recollections (and experiences) of its employees and team members in place of established titles like CEO, VP, GM, or director? What might a team rocker like *farkle* or *over the bars* say about your leadership capability?

Which brings us to the one glaring and distinct difference between riding motorcycles and leadership success.

Motorcycling is extremely unforgiving of inattention, indifference, and arrogance. Leadership sadly and usually is not. We've all experienced it. Micromanagers who can't seem to get out of the way. Self-promoters who take credit for team wins. Blame shifters who point at others when the wheels come off. While these personalities often seem to thrive in business; fortunately, they don't last long.

I recently led a group discussion and asked participants to list their worst experience as a member of a team. The responses included the following:

- No clear vision

- Lack of motivation

- Poor communication

- Unclear structure

- Lack of trust and respect

Every team journey has obstacles in the road ahead: tricky twists and turns, hazardous conditions, and even occasional roadkill. Leadership should not be one of those obstacles. There are many things you can't control when you ride. You can control *how* you ride, *who* you ride with, and *where* you want to go.

I've had the opportunity to develop three successful companies alongside some amazing people who were exceptional leaders: smart, capable, and always ready to serve the team. I also have wasted time remaining too long in some of the most toxic environments with business partners who believed past achievement guaranteed continued success and worked alongside executives so isolated by hierarchy they never looked to see a team struggling with daily "boots on the ground" challenges.

For a time, each of those organizations were "accidentally successful"—acquiring amazing talent but failing to develop and nurture a consistent team culture. Faced with their own limited sustaining capacity and unwilling or unable to change, the "leaders" in charge resorted to the only thing they knew how to do: micromanage and maul. The resulting confusion and disruption eventually wrecked these businesses. Morale crashed, and productivity tanked. All that amazing talent voted with their feet and walked out the door to find opportunities and success elsewhere.

Employment exit polls from Forbes and Gallup make this quite clear: people don't quit companies; they quit bad leaders, almost 50 percent according to the most recent data. Tuning up your organization's leadership practices and techniques is like routine maintenance on a motorcycle. It should never be neglected. In his groundbreaking book, *Zen and the Art of Motorcycle Maintenance: an Inquiry into Values,* author Robert M. Pirsig explains it this way: "The real cycle you're working on is a cycle called yourself."

Scheduling regular leadership "tune-ups"—individually and collectively—provides the power a team needs to manage change, maintain balance, and master capability. That's important because most motorcycle problems are typically caused by the *mechanism* that connects the handlebars to the seat. That mechanism is the rider, or in a team environment, the leader.

A motorcycle isn't something you *have;* it's something you *do.* It's the same thing in leadership. You don't *own* it; you *do* it, employing balance, sound judgment, and good timing to be successful.

Knowing where you want to go, how to get there, and why it matters to everyone involved makes all the difference.

The late great motorcycle daredevil Evel Knievel said it best: "Anybody can jump a motorcycle. The trouble begins when you try to land it."

CHAPTER 6

# ON THE ROAD— THE ATLANTIC SEABOARD (KSU!)

Full-Throttle Leadership Rules of the Road:

> On a motorcycle, you never hear, "Are we there yet?"

From the Full-Throttle Leadership Ride (FTLR) Blog

Key West, Florida, to St. Augustine, Florida, to Niagara Falls, New York—2,861 miles

Thursday, July 4, 2013

Day 7: Key West, FL, to St. Augustine, FL—569 Miles

HAPPY 4TH OF JULY!

Hot! Hot! Hot! Don't get me wrong. After all the rain, I was happy to be dry for a change, but today was blazing. Probably should have known something was up when one of the first streets I came across was named Stickey Way.

Since today's route took me close to Daytona Beach, I couldn't help but remember when my good friend Jason Roberts rolled out of Dallas on a COLD and ICY day back in 2003 for his first trip to Bike Week. He was wrapped head to toe in every layer of cold weather gear he owned or could borrow, resembling the Michelin Man on a Motorcycle. A rookie ride but certainly Good Times!

Arrived in St. Augustine and had a great time walking around the oldest city in the US. My hotel was close to the St. Augustine Lighthouse and Museum, which is worth a visit. Later, caught a bit of the Town's Fireworks Display off The Bridge of Lions. A good day.

Day 8: Friday, July 5, 2013/St. Augustine, FL, to Charleston, SC—376 Miles

I have literally run down one side of Florida and back up the other, and I hope to leave the rain behind me as I leave the state today. My first mechanical glitch of the trip occurred today. While wiping down the bike, I notice my horn had separated from its housing. No lock nut to be found, so rigged it best I could and hit the road.

A working horn, however, is not a luxury item on the highways and byways on the Edge of America, and especially important on a holiday weekend. Stopped at Golden Isles Harley-Davidson in Brunswick, Georgia, for a quick repair. Friendly and Fast!

Passing through Pooler, Georgia, I came across the National Museum of the Mighty Eighth Air Force. I love WWII aircraft, so I had to stop. The Eighth Bomber Command (Re-designated 8th AF in February 1944) was activated on January 28, 1942, at Hunter Field in Savannah, Georgia. During World War II, under the leadership of Generals Ira C. Eaker and Jimmy Doolittle, The Mighty Eighth compiled an impressive record, but their success carried a high price. The 8th AF suffered one-half of the U.S. Army Air Forces' casualties in World War II (47,000-plus casualties with more than 26,000 deaths). The Eighth's personnel also earned 17 Medals of Honor, 220 Distinguished Service Crosses, 850 Silver Stars, 7,000 Purple Hearts, and 46,000 Air Medals.

Entering South Carolina, I was just a few miles away from Marine Corps Recruit Depot Parris Island (MCRD PI). Since I'm wearing a pair of The Boot Campaign's signature Marine boots on the FTLR, I'm also throwing a salute to Brigadier General Lori Reynolds, Commanding General, Eastern Recruiting Region (MCRD PI) and her staff. A little MCRD PI trivia: male recruits living east of the Mississippi and female recruits from all over the United States report here to receive their initial Marine Corps training.

ALMOST made it all the way to Charleston, but the rain still found me. Just a few miles out, and I got soaked again. Stayed overnight with my cousin Amy, her husband Jay, and even got to see my Aunt Judy. Finally, some family to have dinner with!

Day 8 is dedicated to Lloyd W. "Fig" Newton, a retired Air Force four-star general who served as Commander, Air Education and Training Command (COMAETC) from 1997 to 2000. He was also the first African American pilot in the Air Force's Thunderbirds. Note: you can learn a lot by paying attention to the dedication signs posted along our nation's highways!

Day 9: Saturday, July 6, 2013/Charleston, SC, to Norfolk, VA—540 Miles

Left South Carolina, passing through North Carolina and Virginia. I'm beginning to really notice the number of Purple Heart Highways, US Armed Forces Highways, and Blue Star Highways, which are dedicated to our military.

It's a good thing to remember our veterans with memorials. I also think it's just as important to give back NOW to our nation's military members, veterans, and families who have earned our respect and support. So today, go to The Boot Campaign's website—www.bootcampaign.com—and order your own pair of its signature "Give Back" combat boots. Your purchase will help aid in five distinct support initiatives: Housing, Jobs, Wellness, Urgent Assistance, and

Family Support. There's even a place to let them know you heard about Boot Campaign from The Full-Throttle Leadership Ride.

Thanks to Jeff Brady and The Texas Daily on KTXD-TV in Dallas for the interview on The Full-Throttle Leadership Ride. Tomorrow, back on the bike as the FTLR heads to New York City and a special visit to the 9-11 Memorial.

Day 9 is dedicated to Navy SEAL (retired) Marcus Luttrell for his inspiration and to every living recipient of the Purple Heart, established as the "Badge of Merit" by George Washington in 1782.

Day 10: Sunday, July 7, 2013/Norfolk, VA, to New York City, NY—476 Miles

Passed through five states today, beginning with some terrific views of the eastern Shore of Virginia. Paid my FIRST $13.00 toll first of the trip, riding over the Chesapeake Bay Bridge (and through the tunnel) for some great views of the coastline into Maryland and Delaware. Very pretty countryside.

And then a LONG day of construction delays found me. Not sure why construction is being done on Sunday, but every mile offered up new challenges, either a change in route or long, slow, standstill traffic. Not fun.

And then I hit the New Jersey Turnpike, which I highly recommend avoiding at ALL costs. Construction + slow-moving traffic + HEAT = the most miserable day on a motorcycle ever, three hours to cover 117.2 miles. Thank goodness for the roadside service areas. Never so glad to find an exit sign.

Arriving in New York was a welcome relief. Drove over the Verrazano Bridge and the Brooklyn Bridge. I HIGHLY recommend The Best Western Plus Seaport Inn Downtown on Peck Slip. Great property and my room had a large balcony with a terrific view of downtown. A very nice surprise.

Since I was about 2 hours overdue in arriving (still chafing from the New Jersey Turnpike ride), I had just enough time to make it for an interview at the 9-11 Memorial Site. This is a MUST-SEE for all Americans, and overwhelming is the only word for the experience standing at Ground Zero. This national tribute of remembrance pays honor to the men, women, and children killed in the terror attacks of September 11, 2001, and February 26, 1993.

12 years later and I witnessed many expressions of emotion on the faces of the people there. I too was awestruck standing on this sacred ground representing my family, my country, and the Cause, which The Full-Throttle Leadership Ride is supporting. I'll come back here again.

Day 10 is dedicated to the nearly 3,000 people killed in the terror attacks of September 11, 2001, at the World Trade Center site, near Shanksville, Pa., and at the Pentagon, as well as the six people killed in the World Trade Center bombing in February 1993. Their names, along with those who were killed in the 1993 attacks, are inscribed into bronze panels edging the Memorial pools, a powerful reminder of the largest loss of life resulting from a foreign attack on American soil and the greatest single loss of rescue personnel in American history.

Day 11: Monday, July 8, 2013/New York City, NY, to Boston, MA—330 Miles

Made an unscheduled stop in Boston and very glad I did. After the long ride to New York, I needed a shorter day. It ended up being one of the best visits of the Ride.

Stayed in another interesting hotel, The Best Western Plus Roundhouse Suites. This unusual round building was built in the 1800s as a reservoir for the natural gas used to light the streetlamps of Boston. The staff was terrific, and the room was a winner. I like finding these out-of-the-way accommodations.

Immediately headed off to the John F. Kennedy Presidential Library, dedicated to the memory of our nation's thirty-fifth president and to all those who, through the art of politics, seek a new and better world. Anyone who knows me knows that JFK is one of my leadership heroes, so visiting this museum on the FTLR was something special. The Museum has some interesting featured exhibits, including the Mercury Freedom 7 capsule, which carried U.S. Navy Commander

Alan B. Shepard Jr. into space on May 5, 1961, the first American-manned adventure into space.

Also a must-see is "To the Brink: JFK and the Cuban Missile Crisis," a look back from the 50-year mark at excerpts 43 hours of secret recordings relating to the Cuban Missile Crisis, as well as original documents, artifacts, and photographs from the National Archives relating to this milestone 20th-century event.

Later, I went downtown to the site of the recent Boston Marathon bombing, and though many of the flower and candle tributes have been removed, there are still some "Boston Strong" mementos remaining, including the iron fence surrounding a local church with hundreds of colored ribbons left by locals and visitors. Each ribbon had something written on it: a prayer, a name, a remembrance.

The last two days in New York and Boston has reminded me why America continues to thrive during all our challenges and often very petty divisions. There is much that tries to divide and defeat us, but the American Spirit of helping one another, standing together, and identifying as Americans FIRST will always see us through dark days and divisions.

Day 11 is dedicated to the members and families of my home HOG Chapter, the American Eagle HOG Chapter in Corinth, Texas, who have served and are serving in the military. Thank You for your service.

Day 12: Tuesday, July 9, 2013/Boston, MA, to Niagara Falls, NY—570 Miles

Today I am reminded of one of my favorite singer-songwriters, James Taylor. His song "Sweet Baby James" is playing, appropriately, on the iPhone as I wing my way from Massachusetts to New York through the Berkshires. This part of the country is green, deep, rich, and growing. The mist rolls in during the morning, and everything smells wet and alive.

A storm moved in for the last 45 miles to Niagara Falls. Putting on the rain suit, especially on the side of the highway as you watch a storm brewing somewhere down the road in front of you, is a challenging but necessary part of riding a motorcycle.

Like so many aspects of Leadership, doing what we must do—especially the inconvenient or disruptive—is what separates the Best from the Rest. Who knew a rain suit could inspire a leadership lesson?

Arrived in Niagara Falls, NY and headed—where else?—to the Falls. I've been here before, the last time with Wendy, and our dear friends Betty and Gene Garrett back in August 2002 (although then we experienced the Falls from the deck of the Maid of the Mist on the Canadian side). The view here never fails to inspire. Mother Nature is one Awesome Lady!

Staying an extra day to R&R, both for me and the bike. Thanks to the staff at American

Harley-Davidson for the friendly service and the FIRST oil change of the FTLR. Tomorrow, the Ride turns west to Chicago.

Day 12 is dedicated to Boot Girl Char Fontan Westfall and her late husband, Jacques Fontan (Navy SEAL), one of the 19 men who lost their lives in Operation Red Wings on June 28, 2005. I did my Boot Campaign volunteer briefing with Char, and although I didn't know her personal story at the time, I am deeply moved by her sacrifice and continued service to our troops. It's what the Full-Throttle Leadership Ride is all about. Read her story, "Operation Red Wings: A Widow's Perspective" at https://www.bootcampaign.org/operation-red-wings-a-widows-perspective/.

WWII Veterans Tom Blakey (l) and Bert Stolier (r) shared life lessons of service and sacrifice over Sunday breakfast in New Orleans. They were both living examples of the singularly essential quality every great leader must possess, and more importantly; be able to inspire in others, passion.— Photo courtesy of The National WWII Museum

The Original Boot Girls (OBGs), l-r; Ginger Lee, Leigh Ann Ranslem, Sherri Reuland, Heather Scholl and Mariae Bui provided Americans an opportunity to express their patriotism and provide meaningful support to veterans, and it all began with a "Freedom Selfie" in a pair of combat boots. Photo courtesy of The Boot Campaign

Generating awareness and support for veteran wellness and transition programs was, and is, so very important. One of the many interviews from the Full-Throttle Leadership Ride took place at the San Diego Harley-Davidson Dealership, thanks to the efforts of "Boot Girl" Char Ekoniak, San Diego HD owner "New York Myke" and KGTV military reporter Bob Lawrence.—Photo by Author

It all began with a book; "Lone Survivor: The Eyewitness Account of Operation Redwing and the Lost Heroes of SEAL Team 10" by Marcus Luttrell, and a pair of combat boots. Both are a powerful example of what anthropologist and activist Margaret Mead was referring to when she said, "Never doubt that a small group of thoughtful, committed citizens can change the world; indeed, it's the only thing that ever has."—Photo by Author

Ready to Roll! I had accepted a much bigger challenge than just riding around America on a motorcycle; my goal now was to influence everyone I met along the way to live out The Boot Campaign's mission, "When They Come Back, We Give Back."—Photo courtesy of The Boot Campaign

"Overwhelming" is the only word for the experience standing at Ground Zero. The names of the nearly 3,000 people killed in the terror attacks of September 11, 2001 at the World Trade Center site, near Shanksville, Pa., and at the Pentagon, as well as the six people killed in the World Trade Center bombing in February 1993 are inscribed into bronze panels edging the Memorial pools, an emotional tribute to the largest loss of life resulting from a foreign attack on American soil and the greatest single loss of rescue personnel in American history.—Photo by Author

The first time I learned 22 veterans die by suicide each day in our country; opening the morning's issue of The Billings Gazette to find a front page story about a local boy and Army veteran, 23-year-old Wade Christiansen, who took his life on May 29 in the middle of main Street in Bozeman, Montana. The story, entitled "Wounds of War: Injured soldier's death by suicide reflects national issue" was a staggering awakening to a national tragedy we cannot allow to continue.—Photo by Author

I am always struck with a sense of humility and gratitude when visiting a national military cemetery. High above San Diego at Fort Rosecrans National Cemetery, those feelings were even more powerful while paying respects to two of our nation's finest, teammates killed in action just days apart in 2006 in Ramadi. Iraq; Aviation Ordnanceman 2nd Class (SEAL) Marc Alan Lee (August 2, 2006), the first Navy SEAL to lose his life in Operation Iraqi Freedom, and Master-at-Arms Second Class (SEAL) Michael A. Monsoor (September 29, 2006), who received the Medal of Honor posthumously for heroism while serving with SEAL Team 3.— Photo by Author

Riding along a stretch of I-94 in Montana named for native son and Medal of Honor recipient Donald Jack Ruhl, USMC (July 2, 1923–February 21, 1945), who sacrificed his life by falling on a grenade to protect fellow Marines during the Battle of Iwo Jima. Stopped in Butte for lunch and visited with some other local heroes, the members of the Butte-Silver Bow Fire Department, who presented me with their unit challenge coin. One hour later I watched these same first-responders assisting helicopter fire teams battle a huge mountain wildfire, attacking the flames from overhead and on-the-ground, loading water from the river right along the highway.— Photo by Author

Just outside Coos Bay is the David Dewett Veterans Memorial, a focal point for Patriotism, Pride and Remembrance, and a living memorial dedicated to all who have, are or will wear the uniforms of the United States Military. Reading the names on the memorial bricks was especially moving. Just another reminder that honoring our veterans and active duty military is what the Ride is all about.—Photo by Author

From Mobile, Alabama to Big Sur, California - literally from "sea to shining sea"—I visited some of our Country's most iconic natural wonders; including Niagara Falls. The view here never fails to inspire. Mother Nature is one Awesome Lady.—Photo by Author

The Battleship USS ALABAMA (BB-60) sits in Mobile Bay, my boyhood hometown. I've visited her many times over the years, but she's absolutely spectacular at night.—Photo by USS Alabama Battleship Memorial Park

US 1 has to be the best ride on the planet with some of the most amazing "twisties" you can imagine. And the morning view along the rugged coastline winding through Big Sur just takes your breath away.—Photo by Author

Key West, the Southernmost Point in the U.S. To get here I rolled down US 41, The Tamiami Trail, also known as Alligator Alley, through the Heart of the Florida Everglades.—Photo by Author

Part of motorcycle riding is being completely, and at times unpredictably, exposed to the elements. Riding around the Edge of America I encountered scorching summer heat, numbingly cold thunderstorms, the smoky haze of a mountain wildfire and even spotted Big Foot; all the while constantly dodging bugs, dirt and distracted drivers.—Photos by Author, Jcpjr and Janice Williamson

The ride through the Redwood National Forest took me across miles of ancient, majestic trees that reach to heaven along the aptly-named Avenue of Giants. Fog and mist swirl all around, with sun beams streaming through. It's primordial.—Photo by Author

This pair of Boot Campaign military boots were laced up for every mile of the Full-Throttle Leadership Ride. They walked on the sacred ground of National Cemeteries, across grinders and PT grounds at military bases and into the homes of Gold Star Families. They were a daily reminder of how blessed we are to have men and women willing to put their "boots on the ground" to keep our nation free, safe, and strong.—Photo by Author

Since 2013 even more miles have been logged in support of the Boot Campaign, including the Mile Wide Ride in 2017 where I was designated the "Civilian Oversight" for a group of veterans that included Johnny Joey Jones (USMC), Dewaine Hill (USA), John Hindy (USMC) and Jake Schick (USMC). On this day we rolled into the Georgia headquarters of the Zac Brown Band with the Grim Guardians MC.

The "Ride" continues with new experiences to serve, like sharing a stage in Detroit with a group of Gold Star Mothers and Military Families honoring their sacrifice, accompanying WWII veteran John Seelie back to Hawaii for the 74th Anniversary Remembrance at Pearl Harbor and spending an afternoon at NAB Coronado watching a bunch of hopefuls trying to become Navy SEALs. I'm more than blessed.

Being part of the Boot Campaign Tribe has transformed my focus and direction, personally and professionally. Today, I am so grateful for all the miles and memories we've shared together to support veterans and military families. And it just keeps getting better. Join the Ride at www.bootcampaign.com.—Photos by Author

CHAPTER 7

## POWER—FUEL YOUR RIDE

Full-Throttle Leadership Rules of the Road:

> You don't wait for the storms to pass. You learn to
> ride in the rain.

"Passion don't feed the baby!"

A favorite expression of Southern grandmothers. This is absolutely one of my favorite words of wisdom as it perfectly captures the pragmatic outlook you need in life and leadership, which is about confronting and solving challenges. Passion is important, but conditions change. Then what?

Each of us faces obstacles that suck away our energy and focus, and that's when the rubber really does meet the road. It happened to me in the first week of the Full-Throttle Leadership Ride, facing the most severe weather I ever encountered on a motorcycle in the thunderstorm capital of the US.

Florida holds that dubious title, and the summer is a particularly active time of the year for powerful thunderstorms throughout the state. The morning skies were already dark along the Gulf Coast as I left Apalachicola. By noon, conditions rapidly worsened with walloping high winds and detonating bolts of cloud-to-ground lighting directly in my path. Inching along in dangerous conditions and with few places to seek cover, doubt finally flooded in at 430 feet above Tampa Bay crossing over the cable-stay Sunshine Skyway Bridge.

Passion didn't strengthen a numbed hand weakened from constantly gripping a slippery throttle nor inspire confidence as bigger and faster-moving vehicles pitched waves of water directly into my path. Through the distorted lens of a foggy helmet face shield pummeled by thunderstorms, the only thing I could clearly see was I didn't have enough "passion" to keep grinding forward.

With each slow roll of miles on the odometer, my passion washed away in the wickedly fierce Florida weather. In *that* moment, I needed something more to make it through the day. I needed fuel.

I needed *power!*

Power, in this case, is the ability (and responsibility) to direct or influence behavior (yours and others) through the development of skill and proficiency. In life and leadership, developing your skill and proficiency are the tools necessary to be successful every day—strength, dedication, judgment, and grit. When the unexpected occurs (and it always does) and resources fail (and they always will), you need to fall back on something more reliable to fuel a sustainable ride.

Power equals potential. Acquiring the skills and perfecting the techniques to meet whatever challenges arise answers the following.

Think of leadership development as an organization's internal engine. Checking your leadership practices and techniques is as important as routine engine maintenance; it should never be neglected. Tuning up the leadership skills of each team member pushes everyone to grow outside their regular practice and routine.

Nothing is more important to your success because no matter how well you plan, at some point, the tank will run low, the wheels will come off, conditions will change, and you will need to "get off the bike" and reassess the situation. That's how skilled riders change the outcome in their favor.

Skill and proficiency inspire confidence, drive better decision-making, improve performance, and are extremely powerful predictors of your ability to outperform both the competition and circumstances aligned against you. Passion for riding and giving back didn't keep me on the bike during that challenging fourteen-hour, five-hundred-mile gut check when every unpredictable element was screaming, "Quit!" Instead, my training and experience took over.

On the day he was assassinated in Dallas, President John F. Kennedy had a speech prepared for invited guests and local dignitaries at the Trade Mart, outlining the qualities of successful leadership. Known as the *"Undelivered Speech—Nov. 22, 1963,"* President Kennedy wrote, "Leadership and learning are indispensable to each other."

A leader is first and always responsible for the fuel in the tank. That's *how* leadership works.

The right people with the necessary skills, knowledge, and experience—regardless of their place in the pod—make any organization better. That's sustainable success. The very best organizations prioritize learning as a critical component of leadership development and business growth. They are ready when conditions change and challenges arise.

In biker terms, expect to get wet!

In 1997, just two years after we were married, my wife, Wendy, and I were presented with an opportunity to own and operate a business together. On paper, the business was an established success with a past reputation for outstanding customer service. *On paper.* The reality was much different. The small family-owned operation had been poorly managed for several years, losing market share to new competitors, burning out employees, and delivering a substandard experience.

We quickly determined everyone had to be all-in if we were to have any chance of turning the business around. That meant ego, title, and tenure had to go, along with most of the inherited staff. Within a few months, Wendy and I found ourselves starting from scratch with a just a few employees hoping to become a team and make this new venture more successful than ever.

But on a bike or in business, hope is not a strategy.

Because everyone was going to have to do more, we began looking for opportunities for our team members to develop the skills they would need to be successful and accountable. We invested in training, professional certifications, and memberships in industry associations—anything we could think of to provide the fuel (power) to help each member of the team get where we all wanted go. Everyone pitched in; and no job was too big or too small.

It wasn't easy, and early on, we failed often. But we always "got back on the bike" and moved forward together. Eventually, by developing company processes and procedures, we created an identity everyone could be proud of, earning a reputation for both customer service and employee support.

Within three years, every aspect of the business has been restructured: operations, sales and marketing, food and beverage, and event production. Sales increased by one million dollars and company profits by 125 percent. We made it! Times were good.

Then September 11, 2001, happened. Business fell off dramatically and remained that way for another year.

But because we built an organization powered by individuals who had the skills, experience, and a sense of ownership for the success *they* had created, Wendy and I made a business decision to cut operating costs where we could but not team members. Everyone kept their job; we just did what we already knew how to do—pitch in and take care of the customer and one another. We had developed the power to make it through this latest storm. And we did it together.

Six years later, company revenues reached an all-time high of four million dollars.

I often look back on those first years as the most challenging as a business owner, but also the most rewarding and informative. Developing power, skill, and proficiency provided opportunities for each one of us to find our place in the pod and fuel the success we wanted to achieve. We became strong, dedicated, smart, gritty leaders with the power and potential to be successful beyond anything we could have imagined when we started out together in that dysfunctional and failing business back in 1997.

Acquiring the skills and refining the methods to meet whatever challenges come along takes time, commitment, and complete dedication to the journey ahead. It fuels the tank for success.

Here's *how* we did it:

- *Share the lead.* I placed a sign in our conference room that read, "If you think you're the smartest person in the room, you're in the wrong place." Think about *we* and not *me*.

  By sharing the lead, you build a team of people who can run circles around any obstacle they encounter, making everyone exponentially more able, adaptable, and accountable. That's why bikers rotate positions throughout the pod during a group ride. You can't stay out front all the time; there's too much resistance and roadkill along every mile. Changing *your* position in the pod provides new perspectives on just how much your success depends on every member of the team.

- *Show the value.* Take time to appreciate where you've been and who helped get you there. It's important to throttle down occasionally and take in the view. Celebrate where you've been together. Let everyone know why their participation in the journey and on the team is so highly prized.

   Author and motivational speaker Jim Rohn says, "You are the average of the five people you spend the most time with." I know this to be true. Invest in people. Appreciate and recognize their contributions. It absolutely will make you and the organization better.

- *Shut up and listen.* John Wayne gave the best description of a bad "leader"—"short on ears and long on mouth." Make the voice of others as important as your own. The most basic and powerful way to grow leadership is to listen to and learn from others.

   Most people think you need position or authority to be influential. Not true. I've learned many remarkable leadership lessons just listening to and observing people who probably have no idea the powerful impact they've made in my life. So much of the leadership we experience today—in business, in politics, and on social media—is loud, incessant pomposity. Show me a "leader" who does more talking and ordering than listening and learning, and I'll show you a no-growth, failed-leadership environment.

Bikers refer to cars as *cages*. The people strapped inside those steel cubes are boxed in—confined and disconnected. That's also how most organizations operate when it comes to leadership development: a complete time-killing, soul-sucking pathological adherence to tired hierarchy, roles, and responsibilities. Everyone just stays in their lane. No one feels truly empowered. There's no lasting success or sustainability in that ride.

The team with the necessary fuel finishes the ride. When the road gets bumpy, the team capable of responding to the challenge of the moment based on readiness (skills) rather than roles gets back on the bike.

The people around you matter. They're all that really does.

One Team, One Ride.

That's powerful!

CHAPTER 8

# ON THE ROAD—THE INTERNATIONAL BORDER (KSU!)

Full-Throttle Leadership Rules of the Road:

There are *no* shortcuts to any place worth going.

From the Full-Throttle Leadership Ride (FTLR) Blog

Niagara Falls, New York, to Portland, Oregon—3,386 miles

Thursday, July 11, 2013

Day 14: Niagara Falls, NY, to Chicago, IL—769 Miles

Hit the Road early today for the longest stretch of mileage to date. Nice COOL weather for riding to start the morning. Passed through three states: Pennsylvania, Ohio, and Indiana. Lots of farms. It's good to see things growing. I am reminded that some of our nation's soldiers also grew up on the farms and in the small towns across these Heartland states. On a long day like today, it's a reminder of who I'm out here riding for and why they matter.

I'm trying to make up some time, so its "gas and go" most of the day. That doesn't mean you can't learn a few things along the way. Passed through Elkhart, Indiana, home to the RV-Manufactured Housing Hall of Fame and Museum. And if you're wondering, 338 industry pioneers and leaders have been inducted into the RV-MH Hall of Fame since it opened in 1972. If they take nominations from the public, I'm offering up George Roberts (Jason Roberts' Dad) who has been touring the country exclusively in his RV for several years now.

Day 14 is dedicated to President Dwight D. Eisenhower. For many days now, I've noticed highway signs designating the Eisenhower Interstate Highway System. It is named for the former president and Army general who championed its formation on this day in 1954.

Day 15: Friday, July 12, 2013/Chicago, IL, to St. Paul, MN—424 Miles

Left Illinois to cross into Wisconsin. I can see why my HOG friends Bruce and Ruth Gibson are always raving about this state and why Meetings Industry Guru Janet Sperstad calls it home. Met some of the friendliest people at lunch and fuel stops along the way here, and all took some of my Boot Campaign material. There are, however, many, many signs along the roads dedicated to "Cheese" (seriously!).

Today's salute goes to the Wisconsin National Guard Museum at Camp Williams/ Volk Field. It has a great collection of historic aircraft, tanks, and self-propelled guns all on display in an outdoor park setting.

Beautiful, warm, and sunny day to Ride. May be my last for a few days as the weather forecast for Bismarck, Billings, and Coeur d' Alene (next three stops) doesn't look promising.

Day 15 is dedicated to the soldiers of the 56th BSTB Army National Guard from Irving, Texas. We were proud to share Christmas with their families at Circle R Ranch before the soldiers deployed to Iraq in 2010, and they carried the ranch flag with them to fly over the mess hall there.

Day 16: Saturday, July 13, 2013/St. Paul, MN, to Bismarck, ND—549 Miles

The day started gloomy with heavy rains throughout the area. Thought I might have to postpone a day, but the skies cleared just enough for me to chance a run with a late departure. The overcast skies were a perfect setting for all the lakes in Minnesota, and being a gambler, I left without putting the rain suit on. This time, the gamble paid off.

For most of the Ride, other motorcycles have been few and far between, but once I hit North Dakota, I started seeing LOTS of other bikers. I finally feel like I'm part of the community again. Stopped for lunch in Fargo. "Oh, Yah!" Just couldn't help listening for that unique dialect from the movie of the same name, and "Oh, Yah," they do talk like that around here. Pretty funny.

A bit of Road Trivia: Fargo is home to the Roger Maris Museum—signs along the highway call Roger "The Unquestioned Home Run King"—as he hit his sixty-one home runs in 1961 without benefit of performance enhancing drugs, setting a new major league record at the time by breaking Babe Ruth's previous mark of 60 hit in 1927. The day that started so dreary ended up sunny and warm. Maybe the weather will continue this way as I make my way West.

Day 16 is dedicated to the too-many homeless veterans living on the streets of our country, which they served to protect. America's homeless veterans have served in World War II, the Korean War, Cold War, Vietnam War, Grenada, Panama, Lebanon, Persian Gulf War, Afghanistan and Iraq, and the military's anti-drug cultivation efforts in South America. Nearly half of homeless veterans served during the Vietnam era. Two-thirds served our country for at least three years, and one-third were stationed in a war zone. Why don't more Americans know or care about this?

Day 17: Sunday, July 14, 2013/Bismarck, ND, to Billings. MT—527 Miles

So much for the weather hopes. Another rainy, chilly morning and another delayed departure. For the first time on the Ride, I pull on the layers and head toward Montana. Continue to see other bikers, also bundled up, which makes the gloomy skies a bit easier to take. Then I pass several people on bicycles riding along the highway, so I'm not doing any more complaining about the weather. Imagine being caught in a thunderstorm in the middle of nowhere on a bicycle? Rode along The Enchanted Highway where there are some unique sculpture pieces, which dot the landscape. Pretty cool art. Also passed through The Little Missouri National Grasslands and the Theodore Roosevelt National Park. Beautiful.

MONTANA! This really must be God's Country because as soon as I crossed the state line, the skies cleared, the sun came out, and it became one beautiful Big Sky day. The riding in this state will truly take your breath away.

Rode over the Yellowstone River, The Powder River, and The Tongue River and passed by the Little Bighorn Battlefield and the town of Custer. To a boy who grew up reading stories about Buffalo Bill Cody, George Armstrong Custer, Crazy Horse, and Chief Black Kettle, the landscape here conjures up memories of frontier battles and the Wild West.

Just outside Billings is a rock formation called Pompeys Pillar. In July 1806, William

Clark (Lewis and Clark Expedition) passed through the Billings area and carved his name and the date into the rock, leaving the only remaining physical evidence of the expedition that is visible along their route. He named the site after the son of his Shoshone interpreter and guide, Sacajawea. In 1965, Pompeys Pillar was designated as a national historic landmark—one of the smallest in the U.S.—and was proclaimed a national monument in January 2001.

Day 17 is dedicated to U.S. Marine and Afghanistan War Veteran, Alex Minsky. In 2009 while serving in Afghanistan, his truck rolled over an IED, which ultimately resulted in the amputation of part of his right leg. You can see his story of struggle, recovery, and success as a fitness model at ABC News: http://youtu.be/kkbRCqxHxfQ.

Day 18: Monday, July 15, 2013/Billings, MT, to Coeur d' Alene, IA—620 Miles

A bit of a stark departure from my normal posting.

As I was eating breakfast at the hotel this morning, I opened up today's issue of The Billings Gazette to find a front page story about a local boy and Army veteran, 23-year-old Wade Christiansen, who took his life on May 29 in the middle of main Street in Bozeman, Montana. The story, entitled "Wounds of War: Injured soldier's death by suicide reflects national issue" was a powerful reminder of what I'm doing on the

Ride along the Perimeter of the U.S. and why the work of The Boot Campaign is so very important. Nationwide, about 950 veterans attempt suicide every month, with two-thirds succeeding.

According to a national Veterans Affairs study, that's 22 veteran suicides every day in the U.S., a staggering statistic! We don't have to accept tragedies like this, and we CAN do something about it. The Boot Campaign's major area of focus is Veteran Wellness, supporting a full range of treatment and recovery efforts. YOU CAN MAKE A DIFFERENCE TODAY.

I wasn't sure what to expect as I left Billings. Wade's story, so heartbreaking, stood in sharp contrast to this beautiful sunny morning. Everywhere I looked were some of the most inspiring views in our great country. In the distance, I could see Beartooth Mountain, snow still visible on the peaks. At 12,807 feet, Beartooth is the highest point in the state of Montana, and all bikers know that Beartooth Highway (U.S. 212) is one of the best rides anywhere.

Rode along a stretch of I-94 named in honor of Donald Jack Ruhl (July 2, 1923–February 21, 1945), a Montana boy who joined the Marines and sacrificed his life by falling on a grenade to protect fellow Marines during the Battle of Iwo Jima. For his bravery, he was a posthumous recipient of Medal of Honor. Stopped in Butte for lunch and visited with the members of the Butte-Silver Bow Fire Department. All our first responders are heroes too, and it was an honor to hang out with these guys for a while. Took a photo and they even gave me a Department Challenge Coin.

Less than an hour later, I saw, firsthand, how these local firefighters must be ready to respond to an emergency at any moment. Since leaving Butte, the skies in the distance began to darken. Soon I could see a massive smoke cloud billowing and a huge wildfire burning on the mountain. Several fire teams in helicopters and planes were attacking the flames from overhead, loading water from the river right along the highway where I stopped to watch. Stunning images. I couldn't help contrasting the fire burning up hundreds of acres of this area's most valuable resources with the scourge of veteran suicide, which is stealing away the nation's most irreplaceable asset: our Brothers and Sisters who served and sacrificed in combat only to come home and end their lives in despair. Today, I feel empty.

Crossed over into Idaho and finished up perhaps the most emotionally draining day of the Ride.

Day 18 is dedicated to the memory of Wade Christiansen; one of the "22." His brother Matt is sharing Wade's story as a reminder of all the veterans who we've lost to suicide. We can't forget these men and women. We must end this national tragedy.

Day 20: Wednesday, July 17, 2013/Coeur d'
Alene, IA, to Portland, OR—497 Miles

Took a much-needed extra day off the bike.
Ready to get back on the Ride.

Weather forces a change in route as rain
and cloud-to-ground lightning in/around Seattle
make it necessary to detour south, so it's off to
Portland. I leave Idaho and enter Washington,
and within minutes, I know it's going to be a
good ride. Nothing but sunny skies.

Stopped at Rattlesnake Mountain Harley-
Davidson in Kennewick, WA, and left information and flyers on the Boot Campaign. The H-D
HOG Chapters and sponsoring Dealerships
along the route have been so very supportive of
my Ride. Bikers get it!

Not far from the Dealership, I saw an interesting piece of sculpture and stopped to inves-
tigate. Glad I did. It was a 35-foot-tall rem-
nant from the Twin Towers made from three
steel beams that once were part of the World
Trade Center and erected as the city's own 9-11
Memorial. The artifact, weighing nearly 6,000
pounds, was obtained by the city from the Port
Authority of New York & New Jersey. Having
recently visited Ground Zero in NYC and seen
the 9-11 Memorial there, this was another of
those "chicken skin" moments I keep experiencing while on this amazing journey.

Shortly after I headed down I-82 toward
Oregon, crossing over Lake Umatilla on the

Interstate 82/395 Bridge near McNary Dam. I've seen some beautiful parts of this country, but I wasn't prepared for the views along the next 177 miles on I-84. A particularly spectacular section is the Columbia River Gorge, a 4,000-foot-deep canyon, which stretches for over 80 miles winding west through the Cascade Range.

Picture deep-blue winding river waters on the throttle side and towering green mountains on the left, forming a boundary between the Washington to the north and Oregon to the south. As I rode along this awesome creation, I recall a favorite verse from the Bible:

"Who has measured the waters in the hollow of his hand, or with the breadth of his hand marked off the heavens? Who has held the dust of the earth in a basket, or weighed the mountains on the scales and the hills in a balance?" (Isaiah 40:12).

We really do have "spacious skies and amber waves of grain" in many places across our Country. I've seen the "purple mountain majesty and fruited plains" for the past few weeks along the U.S. Perimeter. What a privilege to witness all of this beauty.

Just down the Columbia River Highway is The Dalles, a spectacular historic town located between Mt. Hood and Mt. Adams. The Dalles has a unique place in America's pioneer history; it was the end of the overland Oregon Trail, and Lewis and Clark camped here during their journey to explore the Louisiana Purchase territory in 1805–1806.

A word about Lewis and Clark. I've seen signs along the highway noting their passage through North Dakota, Montana, Idaho, Washington, and Oregon. I've ridden about 1,500 miles through those states, and I can't even imagine walking through some of the rough terrain those explorers crossed. Amazing. (Just so you know, Aubrey and Conor Foster; there's a written report to Dad about the Lewis and Clark Expedition in your future!)

Rolled the last few scenic miles into Portland. Another memorable day AND—The Full-Throttle Leadership Ride has made it to the West Coast!! Will turn south tomorrow for Coos Bay!

Day 20: I'm going to make a departure from my daily dedication to a service member or veteran. Today is dedicated to all of you who have supported The Full-Throttle Leadership Ride with your thoughts, prayers, and contributions. "A journey of a thousand miles begins with a single step," said Chinese philosopher Lao Tzu. My journey began as a bucket list item but has become so much more because of everyone who has supported this effort to honor and serve our military and veterans. THANK YOU. Each of you brought me this far, and I am grateful.

CHAPTER 9

# LEADERS, CHECK YOUR MIRRORS!

Full-Throttle Leadership Rules of the Road:

When you're riding lead, don't spit.

One of the best things about riding motorcycles is the time you get *inside your head.* I often use those moments reflecting on where I've been on my "professional ride" and remembering all the leaders and mentors who thought me worthy of investing time, talent, and treasure in my journey.

No matter where you are going, on a bike or in business, each one of us needs help along the way. None of us becomes successful by ourselves, and anyone who says differently is just arrogantly wrong. So of course, I completely reject the "been there, done that, got here on my own" attitude we experience all the time in so-called leadership. If you've been *there,* someone pointed the way. And if you've done *that,* someone taught you how.

I experienced this early in my career in the person of Col. Edwin C. "Ned" Humphreys, JR. USAF, Retired (1938–1969)[4] who I met in 1978 when he was the publisher and editor of a small weekly newspaper in Mobile, Alabama.

I was looking for a job as a photographer, one for which I was uniquely unqualified for, having no real professional experience other than I enjoyed taking pictures on Kodak instant cameras and the occasional 35 mm borrowed from friends or family. In fact, my only relevant preparation was a twenty-four-hour crash course in film development from my brother Rod (himself an experienced aviation photographer). I'm sure my sister-in-law Joyce was less than pleased when she discovered the toxic chemical spill we left behind in her kitchen, which we converted into a darkroom that evening!

This was long before digital; at that time, film was packaged in rolled canisters and developed in a darkroom using various chemicals. I didn't know how to do that either. Rod was a patient and good teacher. Unfortunately, I was a less-than-prepared student.

So armed with limited skills, boundless ego, and a ridiculous overestimation of my abilities, I headed for my interview at the newspaper with Col. Ned. And I flat out *rocked* our time together. Col. Ned gave me an assignment on the spot, sliding a Yashica Mat 124G camera *(Google it!)* across his desk and sending me out to photograph a high school baseball game. The drive to the high school took just a few minutes, which was helpful because I had never even seen a Yashica Mat 124G camera before. By the time I figured out the box-

---

[4] In 1947, Col. Ned Humphreys founded Bombardiers Inc., an organization dedicated to collecting, recording, and preserving the heritage and tradition of preserving the military profession of bombardiering. That collection now resides in the Office of Air Force History at Maxwell Air Force Base. Col. Humphreys died on April 22, 1996, and was buried with full military honors at Arlington National Cemetery. An honorary plaque in his name is displayed at the National Museum of the US Air Force at Wright-Patterson Air Force Base, near Dayton, Ohio.

STEVEN G. FOSTER, CMP

shaped crank-advance camera is operated by holding it at waist level and looking down into a flat glass viewfinder, the game was already in the sixth inning.

I completed the assignment and headed back to the newspaper office, confident of the praise, and an unprecedented pay raise that certainly must be waiting for me.

On arrival, Col. Ned immediately sent me to develop the film and submit my work. That's where everything changed, and none of it was good.

Inside a pitch-black darkroom, I opened the camera and began to remove the film. My fingers fumbled across something I didn't expect to find: a two-inch-wide roll of 120-mm wooden spool wound with film. My overnight crash course in photography focused entirely on 35-mm format, housed in a small metal container less than an inch wide. I didn't know it, but the film wasn't the only thing about to be exposed.

After several failed attempts to manipulate the film and with any reasonable amount of darkroom time long gone, I did the only thing I could think of to solve my predicament: switching on the small light inside the darkroom—very quickly—just enough to see how to open the strange roll of film and transfer it to a developing canister.

Rule number one in a darkroom: never turn on the light while handling an open canister of film. I exposed the entire roll. I had nothing. And I knew Col. Ned was waiting for me on the other side of the darkroom door. Time to face the music.

"How did it go?" he asked.

I briefly considered trying to bluff my way through failure, blaming a faulty roll of film, diluted darkroom chemicals, a mal-

94

functioning camera, or phantom light streaks inside the darkroom. Instead, I just confessed. "I messed up."

"Yes, you did," said Col. Ned, who then explained my interview hadn't quite been the slam dunk I believed it to be. He knew immediately I was completely unprepared for the job. This was, as we say in Texas; not his first rodeo. My responses to his strategically probing questions had exposed all my fabrications and limitations, especially concerning any skills in darkroom technique and film development, so he sent me out to learn a life lesson I would never forget.

Turns out, the baseball game I was assigned to shoot was a doubleheader, and he already assigned a photographer for the first game. He figured I *might* be able to take the photos, but he really didn't care one way or the other. What he was looking for was how I would respond when exposed as a complete fraud.

Busted, embarrassed, and totally humiliated, I knew the interview was done and the prospect of a job with it. As I rose from the chair, which I had steadily been sinking into for several minutes, Col. Ned said two words that changed my life: "You're hired."

While I was trying to appear not completely dumbfounded, Col. Ned spoke wisdom that any prospective leader and team member should commit to memory. His three simple rules for success were

1. "Ask for help";

2. "Own your mistakes"; and

3. "Change the thing that makes you lie" (that stung and stuck!).

Col. Ned Humphreys was the definition of a full-throttle leader. He was patient, helping every employee push beyond their limitations. Failure was expected, but never accepted. If you owned your mistakes, learned from them, and improved, you were back at it the next day. If not, you didn't stay around very long. He always found ways to encourage and mentor every member of his staff. He helped us get where we wanted to go. And he made sure we arrived there, humble, grateful, and always prepared.

That's become my road map for leadership success.

Today, whenever I hear someone in a leadership position spout their own achievements without acknowledging the contributions of others, I know that person doesn't understand or appreciate the first rule of motorcycling and leadership: "Check your mirrors."

Mirrors are one of the most important parts of a motorcycle. They reflect a thing as it really is in a very clear and accurate way. When riding, constantly scanning back and checking to make sure the pod is moving safely *together* toward the destination is critical to the success of the ride. Checking your mirrors reminds whoever is out front what is most important each mile of the journey—the people trusting your leadership and backing you up.

Developing mirror awareness is central to peak leadership performance. It focuses attention on the elements outside your immediate field of vision, namely everyone following your lead. In a very real sense, the team is the mirror that reflect the leader's sense of responsibility and influence.

Leadership expert John Maxwell says it this way, "A leader is one who knows the way, goes the way, and shows the way."

One of my favorite movies is *Remember the Titans*. It's based on the true story of Herman Boone, an African American high school football coach and his first season at T. C. Williams High School in

Alexandria, Virginia. Coach Boone arrived in 1971 just as the city consolidated all local students into one integrated high school. The entire community was forced to confront racism against the backdrop of the coming football season.

In one powerful scene, Julius, a talented black defensive player, and Gerry, a white defensive player who also is team captain, face off after a grueling series of three-a-day practices. They argue about leadership, unity, trust, and attitude:

> Julius: Why should I give a hoot about you, huh? Or anybody else out there? Nobody plays! Yourself included! I'm supposed to wear myself out for the team? What team? No, No. What I'm gonna do is, I'm gonna look out for myself, and I'm gonna get mine.

> Gerry: See, man? That's the worst attitude I ever heard.

> Julius: Attitude reflects leadership, Captain.

That scene is all about understanding how you got where you are and who helped get you there. Checking your mirrors answers the question, "What is the team reflecting to me?" If you really want to measure your effectiveness as a leader, look at the attitude, skills, and accomplishment reflected by those on the ride with you.

Your focus matters.

CHAPTER 10

# ON THE ROAD—THE WEST COAST (KSU!)

Full-Throttle Leadership Rules of the Road:

> Only a biker knows why a dog sticks his head out of a car window.

From the Full-Throttle Leadership Ride (FTLR) Blog

Portland, Oregon, to San Diego, California—1,769 miles

Thursday, July 18, 2013

Day 21: Portland, OR, to Coos Bay, OR—358 Miles

Got started late this morning. Just needed a little extra time to saddle up. Three weeks and close to 7,000 miles ridden and now 25 states visited. I'm reminded of a "horse-saying" Wendy taught me that's very appropriate at this moment as I feel "rode hard and put up wet."

Left Portland with a nip in the air and sunny skies headed to the West Coast. Crossed over the Willamette River on the Hawthorne Bridge, the oldest vertical-lift bridge in operation in the U.S. One of the memorable parts of this perimeter ride is the many types of bridges I've crossed. This one has a great view of downtown Portland and is on the National Register of Historic Places.

First time riding in Oregon and I am thoroughly enjoying the scenery here: forests of thick jade-green trees, farms, mountains on both sides, deep blue rivers. This is beautiful country.

Turned onto OR-38 (Umpqua Highway) and headed west to the coast. Just one word for the final 75 miles—SPECTACULAR! The two-lane road snakes its way along rugged coastline, through a tunnel cut through the rock, following the Umpqua River. Pulled off the road at Dean Creek to see a large herd of Elk relaxing in a meadow.

Finally made the much-anticipated turn South onto US 101—the Oregon Coast Highway. The Full-Throttle Leadership Ride had finally made it to the West Coast! The last 26 miles took me about an hour to travel; just too many scenic stops for photos, including the Umpqua Lighthouse State Park and Ziolkouski Beach Park.

Just outside Coos Bay is the David Dewett Veterans Memorial, a focal point for Patriotism, Pride, and Remembrance and a living memorial dedicated to all who have, are, or will wear the uniforms of the United States Military. Reading the names on the memorial bricks was especially moving. Just another reminder that honoring our veterans and active-duty military is what the Ride is all about.

Crossed over the McCullough Bridge into Coos Bay. Can't wait to explore it tonight. Tomorrow, off to San Francisco!

Day 21 is dedicated to all the names on the David Dewett Veterans Memorial. Two caught my attention and I posted photos on Facebook: Curtis W. Jenkins, Cpl, USMC, 2001–2005 Iraq; and Tami L. Torgensen, US Army 2-89-7-91, Desert Storm. Thank You for your Service and Sacrifice.

Day 22: Friday, July 19, 2013/Coos Bay, OR, to Oakland, CA—625 Miles

Today's route along US 101 (both the Oregon Coast Highway and into California on the Redwood Highway) was one I had been look-ing forward to since the planning began a few years ago. Spoke to my friend, Kelly Massey, last night about the long day ahead and he answered back, "It will be the best 10 hours you ever spend on a bike."

He nailed it.

Knew the day ahead would be special when I passed Hull Loop Road and Bullard's Beach State Park, reminding me of my riding brother

Doug Hull and long-time friend Cathy Bullard. I had a "Bigfoot" sighting while in the Bandon Marsh National Wildlife Refuge, and there is a photo posted on my Facebook Page for the nonbelievers!

There are so many quaint towns and villages along the Oregon Coast, but had to stop in Port Orford to take a photo (the first of MANY today) of Battle Rock, where the Qua-to-mah Native Americans fought Captain William Tichenor and his men in 1851.

You can hike the hill to the top of the Rock for one of the most spectacular views on the coast and see Grey whales in the cove. The view was incredible and just a peek at what was to come just down the road.

From Battle Rock, through Humbug Mountain State Park, past Sisters Rock State Park, Otter Point, Gold Beach, and Cape Sebastian State Park are miles of beautiful rugged coastline that are simply indescribable (but there are photos on my Facebook Page that may do the actual experience some justice). Every twist and turn along the coastline offered up another breathtaking view; it was difficult not to stop and take photos all day.

Crossed over the Pistol River (I just love the fun names along this road) and over the Chetco River on another of the many bridges I would cross on this journey, headed to the California state line.

I was born in California, at March Air Force Base in Riverside, so riding in my "home state" was something I'd been looking forward to. For years, my friends Gary and Kathleen Vaughan (who reignited my passion for riding motorcycles about 10 years ago) have been telling me about the Redwood Highway, and that it was a "must-ride" for any biker. Their stories, while inspiring, couldn't fully prepare me for my own ride past miles of ancient, majestic Redwood trees that seem to reach the heavens along the aptly named Avenue of Giants.

Fog and mist swirl all around you, with sun beams streaming through primordial, prehistoric titans. Two interesting stops: The Immortal Tree, though not the oldest redwood in the forest, is over 950 years old and stands about 250 feet; and The Tree House, a house partially built within a giant redwood. Awe-inspiring stuff.

I stayed for a while among the Redwoods, just looking at this wonderful creation, which I'm now convinced is "God's Church." This amazingly awesome landscape leaves no doubt.

The rest of the Ride alternated between coastline and forests. This is "postcard country" for sure.

Remember those layers I put on to begin the Ride? By the time I arrived inland later in the day, the temperature had rocketed into the 90s, and it was toasty. Stripped down to normal riding attire and throttled on. The final hours of the ride took me through wine country, acres of grapes and tasting rooms. There really is something for everyone on this stretch of the American Road.

Crossed over the Oakland Bay Bridge and checked in to the hotel. WHAT A DAY!

Day 22 is dedicated to the men and women of the US Coast Guard Group/Air Station in North Bend, OR. "Semper Paratus" (Always Ready).

## Day 23: Saturday, July 20, 2013/Oakland, CA, to Morro Bay, CA—335 Miles

I know I'm out here on a ride of gratitude, but I'm beginning the day with a gripe!

Apparently, in California, the center stripe is an actual lane for motorcycles. Now I've seen some pretty dumb "squid" behavior in my time on a bike: 20-somethings weaving at high speed between vehicles on their way to a certain smash-up, but as my Ladies of Harley friend Suz Awbrey would say, these "crazy Cali driver" have taken bad behavior on a motorcycle to a whole new level. Unbelievable!

Once I left the crazy big city traffic behind, it was on to navigating some of the most amazing "twisties" you can imagine along US 1. Looping sharp turns along coastline, some of it with little or no guardrail (so a distraction here and it's a long way down to the bottom), make winding through Carmel, Point Lobos, Big Sur, and San Simeon—a coastal canvas worth seeing. So many places to stop and take in the spectacular scenery, which I did at every opportunity.

Spotted surfers and elephant seals fighting for the best spot on and off the beach, surrounded by sheer cliff faces and occasionally falling rocks—all under alternating cloudy/chilly and sunny/warm skies. I never hit more than 30 miles per hour—took me almost six hours to make the drive—but it was sure worth it!

Later that afternoon, I arrived in Morro Bay, sometimes called the Gibraltar of the Pacific. It's named for Morro Rock, discovered in 1542 by Portuguese navigator Juan Rodriquez Cabrillo. (You can learn a lot by watching the Hotel Info channel in your room). Checked in and took some time to do mundane road stuff: laundry, wash the bike, eat!

Then headed down to the harbor to catch the sunset. The US Coast Guard lists the harbor as one of the most dangerous in the entire nation. From 1979 to 1987, 21 lives were lost in boating accidents alone, and many additional deaths have resulted from sightseers and fisherman being swept off the rocks of the breakwater surrounding Morro Rock. The Coast Guard was diligently working the harbor that evening.

A beautiful place to catch a sunset, and another outstanding day on the Full-Throttle Leadership Ride.

Day 23 is dedicated to those serving in the National Guard at Camp San Luis Obispo. It also houses the California State Military Museum and serves as a training ground for several local, state, and federal agencies.

Day 24: Sunday, July 21, 2013/Morro Bay, CA, to San Diego, CA—451 Miles

Left early headed down US-101 passing through San Luis Obispo, Santa Maria, and Lompoc. More fertile growing country: vine-yards, strawberries, peaches, and dates fill acres of farmland. Took CA-154 up through the Los Padres National Forest past Lake Cachuma. What a view!

Just out here riding and California Dreaming. Back on US-101 through Santa Barbara and into Ventura (couldn't help singing America's "Ventura Highway") and onto my first BIG city in days—Los Angeles. Drove through North Hollywood near the set of *Sons of Anarchy* (the Teller Morrow Automotive set is on Radford in case you want to visit). Back on the "Crazy Cali" freeway and onto I-5 through Anaheim and Irvine before making it back to the coastline for the drive into San Diego.

Day 24 is dedicated to all the Military and First Responder families. We know you also Serve and Sacrifice. God Bless You.

Day 25: Monday, July 22, 2013/Time off the bike

Took an extra day off in San Diego for some R&R to prepare for the journey home on the final week of the FTLR. Did an interview with Channel 10 News, which aired on the 6 pm ABC broadcast. Thanks to San Diego Boot Girl Char Ekoniak, San Diego Harley-Davidson owner New York Myke, and reporter Bob Lawrence for helping get out the word on the Full-Throttle Leadership Ride.

We talked about two very different encounters with people I met on both ends of the Country.

The first occurred at the 9-11 Memorial in New York City. As I've said in previous posts, my Boot Campaign military boots, which I've worn every day on this adventure, are a sure icebreaker. Most people see them and assume I'm in the military. Whenever I share the story behind the boots and the Ride, the response is always a good one.

This was different. A visitor asked about my boots. I enthusiastically explained the Cause, The Campaign, and the Ride. He listened intently but said he couldn't contribute to the Ride because he didn't support the War in Iraq and Afghanistan. I was surprised by his reaction, especially considering the place where we stood honored fellow Americans who were the first victims of those wars. The ride wasn't about support for a war. It was about saying "thank you" to Veterans and Military Families. It just didn't connect with him.

He walked away without even a wish for "good luck."

The second encounter took place just outside San Diego at a scenic overlook near the Pacific Ocean. This time, a man wearing a Harley T-shirt approached, asked about my bike and where I was going. Once again, I shared my story. He then told me his son was serving in the Army and currently on deployment. He was wearing his son's Army ring, which he said he puts on his finger first thing every morning along with his wedding ring.

We talked for some time: sharing our love for motorcycles and respect for the military, expressing concerns for a country grown apathetic and divided, and what we believed real leadership looks like. After a handshake and one big bear hug, this military Dad said "thank you," reached into his wallet, and offered to give me gas money to continue the trip. Amazing! His son is serving in harm's way, and he is concerned about me having enough fuel to make it to the next stop. I respectfully declined and thanked him again for his family's service to our country.

I've thought often about these two men and their contrasting outlooks—their own "leadership capability," if you will. One placed a high value on his own opinion, confident in a narrow viewpoint that missed the mark. The other was grateful and appreciative, having already invested his most prized "treasure" in something bigger than himself.

Some people get it. They serve and sacrifice. Others don't, prisoners of their own restricting thoughts and beliefs.

I prefer people who get it and challenge limitations rather than surrendering to them.

CHAPTER 11

# PURPOSE—FOCUS YOUR RIDE

Full-Throttle Leadership Rules of the Road:

> Never mistake horsepower for staying power.

I'm old enough to remember a time when my mom warned us to "never accept a ride from a stranger." Today, none of us think twice about jumping in a vehicle driven by a complete and total stranger. We just use an app and order a ride. Technology has changed all of Mom's rules.

We can do almost anything—shopping, banking, travel, dining, and entertainment—with just a *click*. Technology provides us with endless opportunities to do everything faster. It erases borders, extends education, advances health care, and accelerates communication. It also deprives us of the most basic human interactions.

While we can instantly access a "friend's" daily "status" through social media, what's missing are the intricacies involved in having *real*, meaningful relationships. Writing a letter is a lost art. Texting has replaced traditional conversation. Quality time has been redefined.

We're more "connected" than at any time in history. But also less "in touch."

Nowhere is this more obvious than in leadership. We are dazzled by those 128 million internet hits on the topic directing us to the latest theory or iteration on what leadership is supposed to be. Leadership isn't ice cream. The "flavor of the week" rarely satisfies for long.

In Chapter 2, we discussed leadership *capacity* and the differences in what we say we *know* about leadership and what we actually *do* as leaders. I defined successful leadership as using your individual capacity—your IT—to positively influence, impact, and inspire others to achieve something meaningful.

No organization serious about success fails to define IT. Usually, the process begins by categorizing goals, metrics, and bottom-line strategies. Each one is an important component, but not the sustaining element. Because no matter how well you plan the ride, somewhere along the way, something will take you off the bike. Fatigue sets in. Resources fail. The tank gets empty. Roadkill pops up.

So many obstacles lie waiting to disrupt your journey. And it's not a lack of desire (passion), resources (power), or even an abundance of discomfort that often is responsible for most organizational failures.

The one ingredient necessary to get you back on the machine and sustain the ride is *purpose.*

Defining a common purpose helps manage change, maintain balance, and improve communication. Purpose sparks interest and provides encouragement, becoming a compelling force to affect the actions, behaviors, and opinions of others. It offers a team the ability to avoid the burnout and uncertainty, which so often ends up in a heap of twisted perspectives and ruined expectations.

Since 1927, *Time* magazine has chosen a man, woman, or idea that "for better or worse, has most influenced events in the preceding year." The list of eighty-six includes trailblazers, world leaders, cultural icons, and the famous and the infamous. Charles Lindbergh was the first and the youngest person to receive the distinction; which also has included US scientists (1960), American women (1975), the computer (1982), the Earth (1988), and the American soldier (2003). Since the list began, every serving president of the United States has been a Person of the Year at least once except Calvin Coolidge, Herbert Hoover, and Gerald Ford.

*Time* named <u>*You*</u> in 2006 when the magazine recognized the millions of people who anonymously contributed user-generated content to blogs, wikis, social media, and other websites. In every instance where a discovery, cure, cause, or challenge led to positive change, the common denominator was purpose-driven leadership.

Purpose does more than just state "we're all in this together." It replaces doubt, fear, and uncertainty with hope and determination. Purpose makes the load easier to bear. It transforms the moment, filling us with promise, hope, and focus. And for everyone involved—even if that's just *you*—it's an opportunity to move from mundane to meaningful.

People like to come together around a cause. So often, organizations set objectives that may (or may not) produce results for the business but bring absolutely no satisfaction or gain to those people tasked with making it all happen. Purpose defines "what matters most" and creates engagement that is consequential to both the organization and its people.

Purpose provides a route to stand out.

That's exactly what those Original Boots Girls (OBGs) accomplished when they decided to do something meaningful to outwardly express their gratitude for active-duty service members, veterans, and their families. "What overwhelmed me was the feeling I had of 'What now?'" recalls OBG Leigh Ann Ranslem. "Thinking about the sacrifice that members of our military and their families make to keep us safe weighed heavily on me. We all just felt the need to do something."

That *something*—a simple "Freedom Selfie" in a pair of second-hand combat boots—powerfully connected with other people, who saw their own opportunity to "lace up," get involved, and make a parallel and distinctive difference.

An orthodontist, a photographer, a working mom, a personal trainer, and an occupational therapist believed they could provide assistance and support to a cause they cared about. They were willing to take a risk, get creative, and give something back. Their act was organic, even small, but the purpose it ignited in others revealed opportunities beyond anything they could have originally imagined.

Thomas Edison said it best: "If we did all the things we are capable of, we would astound ourselves." And not just that, I believe we would change ourselves and change the world. That's *real* leadership.

Write these words down: *differentiation, intention, loyalty.* These are the undeniable bottom-line benefits any organization can reap from developing a purposeful culture. Many of the companies who regularly appear on lists of the "Best Places to Work"—Southwest Airlines, In-n-Out Burger, Salesforce, Hilton, American Express, and CarMax (to name a few)—define *purpose* as "goodness." They understand that doing *good* doesn't just feel good; it also makes good business sense and adds value to any organization's bottom line.

Traditional leadership thought is to separate the personal from the professional, but organizations, like families, have conflicts to manage, personalities to mesh, and growth to mentor. Here's what the employees from the companies on a recent Forbes 100 list had to say about their organizations' purposeful culture:

- *It's feeling you're part of a family.*
- *There a nonpunitive attitude toward those who make mistakes.*
- *They care with authenticity.*
- *Everyone pulls together—almost like a family.*
- *It's very dynamic, with strong interpersonal relationships.*

Leadership that cares enough to support the development and growth of its people, not just with material needs but also by meeting their personal and emotional needs, creates a dynamic organization built to sustain and succeed in all kinds of situations. Providing balance, common goals, shared responsibility, open communication, commitment, integrity, and a generous, purposeful spirit results in much more than just making a list of great places to work.

They're a family with a purpose, and that's unstoppable.

According to the Cone Communications and Echo Research Study, consumers also feel a personal sense of accountability to be purposeful and actively look to companies as partners in making progress to serve others. Call it what you like—purpose, cause, or giving back. It's not just *big* business; it is *good* business. And according to the survey:

- It is a major point of differentiation;
- It's a leading indicator of customer intention and loyalty;
- 90 percent of consumers would switch to a brand with a cause; and
- 85 percent of millennials correlate purchasing to CSR.[5]

---

[5] The eighty million members of the millennial generation (born 1977 to 1995) represent 25 percent of the US population, and more than two hundred billion dollars in annual buying power and by 2025 will comprise 75 percent of the global workforce.

Purpose builds respect and reputation in the community and shapes meaningful business connections. It encourages morale and commitment and develops knowledge and expertise. Think about it. How much more bottom-line impact could you generate if your organization were recognized as a "purposeful place" that does good by everyone who comes in the front door? How difficult would it really be to make some small purposeful changes today that tell a more compelling story about who you are and entice more people to join your own leadership ride?

Both the *Harvard Business Review* and *Fortune* magazine have written extensively on the impact of purposeful work as a training ground for leadership, accountability, and dedication. Companies that are purposeful offer influential opportunities for their employees to develop leadership skills like problem solving, mentoring, and communication, all of which are instrumental to building and sustaining a successful team environment.

When it comes to purpose, in every sense, "the juice is worth the squeeze!"

CHAPTER 12

# ON THE ROAD—TURNING FOR HOME (KSU!)

Full-Throttle Leadership Road Rules:

> "It's good to have an end to journey towards; but in the end, it is the journey that matters most" (Ursula K. Le Guin).

From the Full-Throttle Leadership Ride (FTLR) Blog

San Diego, California, to San Marcos, Texas—1,851 miles

Day 26: Tuesday, July 23, 2013

San Diego, CA to Phoenix, AZ—482 Miles

Today, the Full-Throttle Leadership Ride heads into its final two weeks. To date, I've logged 10,000 miles through 30 states—more than 3/4s of the Ride is done. WOW!

I head east on I-8 leaving the West Coast, the twisties, mountains, and ocean behind me. Time to turn for Home! The scenery changes quickly; I'm out of the city and into the California Desert before long, passing through the Cleveland National Forest and funky little places in the road like Jacumba, Tecate Divide, and Yuha. And the desert temperature starts to soar.

I pass by a memorial highway marker to Army Sgt. Brud J. Cronkrite, who was KIA on May 14, 2004, while serving during Operation Iraqi Freedom. The 22-year-old soldier was assigned to the 1st Battalion, 37th Armor, 1st Armored Division. He died from injuries he sustained when a rocket-propelled grenade was fired into a nearby building while he was on security patrol in Karbala, Iraq. Another reminder of what I'm out here doing.

The closer I get to the Mexico Border (and I can see it), the hotter it gets. Its 105 degrees on the desert floor, and I'm baking. So glad I purchased that Harley-Davidson cooler from Jonnee Evans at American Eagle Harley before leaving town. That little sucker packed with ice, Gatorade, and a cool towel will save my butt more than once today.

Nearing the border with Arizona, the terrain changes quickly, from rocks to "beach" at the Algodones Dunes, 45 miles long by 6 miles wide of some of the prettiest white sand dunes you'll ever see. Crossed over into Arizona and stopped in Yuma for lunch. I've noted many road signs during the Ride and commented on a few. Passed one today I had not seen in a while: "Elevation Sea Level."

Finished up riding past the Painted Rock Petroglyph Site and just at the edge of the Sonoran Desert National Monument.

Taking tomorrow off to relax in Phoenix and catch up with industry icon and leadership guru, Ed Scannell. Should be another good day.

Today is dedicated to NASA. On this day in 1969, *Apollo 11,* the U.S. spacecraft that had taken the first astronauts to the surface of the moon, returned safely to Earth. I passed several NASA facilities along the way, and since many astronauts have military backgrounds, today the FTLR salutes them.

Day 28: Thursday, July 25, 2013/Phoenix to Las Cruces—523 Miles

Left Phoenix under cloudy skies and a bit of rain, but since I was headed into the desert, the cooler temperatures were a welcome start to the day.

Although I missed my friends with the MPI Arizona Sunbelt Chapter (they were just returning from a conference in Las Vegas), I did blow past the Wild House Pass Casino & Resort where just last month, Judy Webster and I facilitated a chapter board retreat. Interesting to be riding by just a few weeks later!

Stopped at Tucson Harley-Davidson and dropped off more Ride/Boot Campaign materials for their HOG Chapter. The H-D dealerships along the route has been great when it comes to helping me promote the Ride.

Some very interesting side trips and stops today.

The Pinal Airpark just off I-10 is the final resting place for civilian commercial aircraft. Old airplanes are lined up there waiting to be scrapped. Not far away is the 309th Aerospace Maintenance and Regeneration Group at Davis-Monthan Air Force Base that provides the same service for military aircraft. Not a site you see very often, huge commercial jets sitting silently by the roadside alongside private jets, even one once owned by Elvis Presley!

Came within shootin' distance of Tombstone, famous for the Gunfight at the OK Corral between the Earps and Doc Holliday, and a group of outlaws known as The Cowboys.

It didn't take long for those cool morning temperatures to give way to the heat, which was back up over 105 when I stopped at Texas Canyon (AZ) for a break. Saw lots of interesting road signs along the way, especially at roadside rest stops and scenic vistas. If you're ever in the area, pay attention to the ones posted with pictures of rattlesnakes and scorpions, warning to stay off the rocks!

Lots of Wilderness Study Areas and State Parks to pass through as I entered New Mexico. I did stop for lunch near the Shakespeare Ghost Town, so made a short run there and visited the nearby Veterans Park as well.

Probably would have stopped even more if my back tire wasn't WELL past the time for a replacement, so I made my way to Las Cruces and Barnett's H-D for the replacement. Great customer service here; they stayed late to get the work done so I could stay on schedule.

Day 28 is dedicated to my Friend, Gary Woods, and every Vietnam-era veteran (1959–1975). Your service is honored, and we remember the 58,200 names of those who died or are listed as MIA.

Day 29: Friday, July 26, 2013/Las Cruces to Junction—589 Miles

Another one of those "change in plans" to have popped up along the way. Wendy and the Kids decided to meet me tomorrow, so I'm altering the route to spend a day with them in San Marcos, Texas. Not ready to bust out another long, hot, and dusty day on the bike, so I'm headed to Junction, which will put me within 250 miles of them tomorrow.

Leaving New Mexico and crossed over the border to Texas. Stopped at the "other" Barnett's H-D, this one billed as the World's Largest, to check-in with the HOG Chapter there and leave them some Boot Campaign information.

It's great to back in Texas. My home chapter, American Eagle HOG, likes riding in this part of the state, and we've done so many times as part of our annual Lone Star Challenge Points Ride. Passing through Van Horn, Fort Stockton, Balmorhea State Park, and Ozona was like a reunion ride in many ways.

Also drove into Fort Hancock, which is not just a powerhouse in the high school sport of 6-Man Football but also featured prominently in one of my favorite movies, *The Shawshank Redemption*. If you are a fan, Fort Hancock is where the main character, Andy Dufresne, crossed the border into Mexico after escaping from Shawshank Prison on his way to the beaches at Zihuantanejo.

The Texas sunshine is a welcome sight, but the Texas heat played havoc with the bike, baking my heat shields to the point where both literally fell apart. A quick fix and then on to Junction.

The small Texas town played host to a memorable 10-day football camp run by Paul "Bear" Bryant in 1954, his first year as head coach at Texas A&M. The Junction Boys is the name given to the "survivors" of that camp—an ordeal that has since achieved legendary status—and was the subject of a 2001 book *The Junction Boys* and a movie produced by ESPN.

At the time, the Texas Hill Country town was experiencing severe drought and heat, with temperatures soaring over 100 degrees each day of camp. Practices began before dawn, lasting all day with meetings until 11:00 PM. The heat, practice schedule, and Bryant's refusal to allow water breaks was too much for many of the players, and each day, many quit the team.

By the end of the 10-day camp, only a fraction of those that started were left. Among the "survivors" (the number varies from 27 to 35) were future NFL coach Jack Pardee and future Dallas Cowboys coach and Alabama coach Gene Stallings.

Being an Alabama guy, of course, I had to try to find the site of this famous football camp, and I did. Its located just a few miles outside the town. A detour that just adds more memories to my Biker Bucket List Ride.

Day 29 is dedicated to the 1st Armored Division at Fort Bliss, the Army's second-largest installation. I visited the museum on post, and it's a must-see if you're in El Paso.

Day 30: Saturday, July 27, 2013/Junction to San Marcos—257 Miles

Short post for today's ride. Continued down I-10 toward San Antonio and a rendezvous with my family. Haven't seen Wendy in the kids in a month, so coming "off-route" for a few days to just hang out with the Family—what a welcome relief from the road. 30 days is a long time to be away from your family—imagine a full military's tour separation.

Make no mistake; military families also serve and sacrifice. Supporting that community is a major focus for the Boot Campaign. If you want to help, you can make an impact at http:// www.bootcampaign.org.

Today's Ride (and salute!) is dedicated to the men and women at Joint Base San Antonio, the largest base organization in the Department of Defense, comprising three primary locations at JBSA-Fort Sam Houston, Lackland, and Randolph and more than 200 mission partners. JBSA services more DoD students and active runways than any other installation, houses the DoD's largest hospital, and supports more than 250,000 personnel including 425 retired general officers.

# CHAPTER 13

# WIND THERAPY

Full-Throttle Leadership Road Rules:

Four wheels move the body; two wheels move the soul.

Days 32–34: Monday, July 29–Wednesday, July 31/San Marcos, TX, to Argyle, TX—900 Miles

31 Days and more than 12,000 miles in the mirror and nearing the end of my journey. The final route will take me South through small Texas towns (Three Rivers, George West) and down to Corpus Christi. From there, along the Texas Gulf Coast, it's on to Galveston and then a turn North along some familiar roads, Highway 290 and 6, as the John Denver song says, "Take Me Home, Country Roads."

My eyes are on the road Home, but my thoughts, increasingly, turn to my travels on the Edge of America.

I've taken many trips across the country before this one. As a boy, we moved often, so I saw a lot of America from the back seat of several family automobiles. There were also adventure getaways where we loaded up the car and drove to some popular vacation destination. As a young man, I traveled in a van with bandmates to gigs in small towns and big cities, and later, my career moves took me from Alabama to Hawaii. Each trip had its own memories, mischief, and mishaps.

This road trip has been different. The bike made it so. A motorcycle is therapy. It changes your perspective. A motorcycle isn't something you have; it's something you do.

And whatever you do and wherever you go, it's just better in the wind.

There's a sense of adventure that comes by choosing to go off route at the end of a long day just to experience the tantalizing promise of a sign marked "Scenic Vista Ahead." When you ride, you lean into every twist and turn. You see more, smell more, feel more. An errand to the local grocery store for supplies, a dinner ride with your buddies, and certainly a 13,000-mile perimeter ride become a full-body experiences.

Immersed in the elements—rain, wind, sun, chill—you adapt to the always-changing conditions. You're not numbed by artificial climate-control temperatures, disconnected from the road, and distracted by technology. You are present, in the moment, focused, and constantly shifting to a different gear.

Here's another area where leadership and riding a motorcycle connect.

You can't dabble in either. The greater the commitment, the greater the return; and you are successful when you've discovered and delivered ways to create meaningful experiences, purposeful engagement, and arrived at a destination where everyone involved can stand back, take in the view, and express a collective "WOW!"

Leadership is about opening the heart. It is an attitude, not a routine.

I spend a lot of time working with CEOs, HR Managers, and Small Business Owners on a variety of leadership and team issues. Two are ALWAYS at the top of the list: employee engagement and customer loyalty. Most organizations that are not making any real headway in either area all have one thing in common—they are stuck in "Culture Neutral," just riding along in the same direction at the same speed, disconnected and distracted, headed somewhere with no heart.

And no fun.

Yes, leadership (like motorcycling) should be FUN!

So say some of the world's leading neuroscientists who have identified a process called neurogenesis, which occurs when the brain is on positive (having fun) by stimulating cognitive capacity—including intelligence, creativity, energy levels, and memory. Even business outcomes improve; studies showed people having FUN were 37% better at sales than at everyday neutral.

Doesn't earning a rocker from the team like "Fun Boss" or "All-In" read so much better on your professional "Cut" than being tagged as one of the 7 Dwarfs of Failed Leadership—"Nasty, Needy, Clueless, Chaos, Snooty, Shameful, and Me"? If you're serious about leadership, get serious about fueling your ride with passion, power, and purpose (and top off the tank with some fun!).

Doing the same thing over and over again and expecting different results isn't the definition of *insanity*; its *Extreme Foolishness*. To change your leadership outcome, change your leadership outlook.

As leaders, we have to pay attention to everything, understanding there are no quick fixes. To lead is committing to the long run to deliver consistent results, achieve high performance, and manage multiple and often conflicting priorities in service to something greater than your personal set of priorities.

As I get closer to Home, I finally put "IT" together. And it's this:

- Leadership is Worthwhile.

- Leadership is Empowering.

- Leadership is Kind.

- Leadership is Steady.

- Leadership is Inspirational.

That's what I've learned while riding around the Country from people who are fully engaged in their communities: shifting gears, overcoming obstacles, and creating opportunities that make the lives of others better. They are leaning into the wind, embracing the road ahead, and doing what others think is too hard, too time-consuming, or just not worth it.

"When you know who you are; when your mission is clear, and you burn with the inner fire of unbreakable will; no cold can touch your heart; no deluge can dampen your purpose. You know that you are alive" (Chief Si'ahl, Suquamish and Duwamish leader).

CHAPTER 14

# LESSONS LEARNED— THE RIDE CONTINUES

Full-Throttle Leadership Road Rules:

> "The problem is not the problem. The problem
> is your attitude about the problem" (Captain
> Jack Sparrow, Disney's *Pirates of the Caribbean*).

If I'm being honest, I was never so happy to get off a motorcycle than the day I put the kickstand down at home. And if you had asked me in that moment what I would remember most about my time on the bike, I would have replied, "How much my butt hurts!"

I'm not sure time heals all wounds, but it works pretty well on saddle sores, and in the months that followed, I had the opportunity to put the lessons of the Full-Throttle Leadership Ride in perspective. We live in a chaotic, frenzied, technologically fueled world. It provides endless opportunities, unprecedented reach, and on-demand access, but at the cost of the most basic human interactions.

Social media has amped the velocity in which everything is instantly available and virally on demand with a simple click. That makes distinguishing *real* value and substance from the torrent of random images, casual observations, and cultural junk constantly spewing forth a huge challenge for all of us.

Riding across America put me back in touch with America.

It's a country filled with iconic natural wonders, from Niagara Falls to the Redwoods National Forest, and great adventures on roads like Alligator Alley on US 1 down to the southernmost point in the continental US at Key West and along the International Boundary with Canada on the Enchanted Highway from Minnesota to Washington State.

From Mobile, Alabama, to Big Sur, California, I experienced the natural beauty of America from "sea to shining sea."

More importantly, I discovered a sense of belonging in the faces and stories of the remarkable people I met along the way. Their heroism, strength, service, and perseverance, sometimes in the face of overwhelming odds and great loss, reminded me that we all have a duty to one another to get up every day and lace up our own boots, committed to make life better for others.

That's who we are, and that's what leadership is really about.

And because my ride became a cause and not just another meaningless and self-absorbed social-media selfie, something interesting occurred. I began hearing from and meeting people who shared their own Passion-Power-Purpose stories with me. Some were veterans who just wanted to say thank you for my efforts, which was completely humbling, or were involved in their own service projects. There were business professionals who reached out to ask how to connect their organizations' leadership efforts with a sustainable "Goodness" campaign. And fellow bikers, inspired to embark on their own "Cause Ride," requested information on planning and logistics. I didn't expect any of it but am so grateful for all of them.

These extraordinary people, and so many others, continue to inspire me today. I am honored to share a few of their stories with you here. These heroes challenge us all to run full-throttle every day:

- **Cindy Dietz-Marsh** is the Gold Star mother of Petty Officer 2nd Class Danny Dietz, a member of the four-Man SEAL team memorialized in *Lone Survivor*. She also is the author of the book *Danny: the Virtues Within.* I met Cindy and her husband, Vietnam veteran Don Marsh, at a motorcycle ride in San Antonio, Texas, sponsored by the Boot Campaign. We spent the entire weekend together, and before heading home, Cindy gifted me with one of Danny's SEAL team challenge coins.

  To honor their son and brother and all who serve and sacrifice, Cindy and her family started two nonprofit organizations: the Danny Dietz Jr. Foundation (www. dannydietzjr.com) to promote a "Team First" environ-ment designed to create better citizens and members of the community and the Danny Dietz Memorial Fund (www. navysealdannydietz.com), which provides assistance and resources to a variety of veterans organizations.

  Cindy and Don have become close friends, and we've shared a few miles together in the years since, traveling the country together and speaking to individuals and organiza-tions about the importance of service and sacrifice to one's country, family, and community.

- **Corporal Jacob Schick**, USMC (Ret.), is a third gener-ation marine who epitomizes service and sacrifice. After a triple-stacked tank mine detonated below his vehicle in Al Anbar Province, Iraq, in 2004, Jake suffered compound fractures in his left leg and left arm; multiple skin, liga-ment, and bone losses; varying burns; partial loss of his left hand and arm; amputation below the knee of his right leg;

traumatic brain injury (TBI); and post-traumatic stress disorder (PTSD).

He endured forty-six operations and twenty-three blood transfusions, but he will tell you his physical injuries weren't the worst. For years, Jake dreaded his TBI and PTSD diagnosis, a common mind-set among warriors. "Physical pain reminds you you're alive. Mental pain tests your will to stay that way," says Jake, executive director for 22Kill (www.22kill.com), a veteran service organization dedicated to battling veteran suicide.

Also a working actor, Jake was featured in James Gandolfini's HBO special *Alive Day Memories: Home from Iraq* as well as *60 Minute Sports* and had a role in the Academy Award nominated films *American Sniper* and *A Star Is Born*.

- **Krystal Hess**, founder of Motorcycle Missions (www.motorcycle-missions.org), is rebuilding lives every day with the turn of a wrench. A pediatric and surgical nurse who found herself alone and suffering from PTSD after escaping domestic violence in her marriage and witnessing a loved one's suicide attempt, Krystal could have easily surrendered to her circumstances. But among the wreckage of these relationships were a pile of tools and assorted motorcycle parts.

Instead of giving up, she began healing by learning everything she could about motorcycles. Krystal's journey turned personal tragedy into triumph as she developed the skills that eventually led her to becoming an award-winning motorcycle builder and establishing her own business, Ricochet Customs. Understanding how important working on a motorcycle was in rebuilding her own life, Krystal then founded Motorcycle Missions, a nonprofit that provides veterans and first responders the opportunity to come together for support and healing through a unique brand of therapy: building and riding motorcycles.

As the program has grown, Motorcycle Missions bikes have won numerous awards at motorcycle shows. One of her bikes is on display at the Haas Motorcycle Museum in Dallas. More importantly, Krystal has built a place where purpose, camaraderie, and healing is available for those seeking a happy, healthy, and balanced lifestyle after trauma.

- On the streets of Dallas, Texas, people call **David Timothy** "the Soup Man." The founder and executive director of the SoupMobile (www.soupmobile.org), a "mobile" soup kitchen, David and his dedicated team of volunteers have been feeding the homeless since 2003. Their mission is a ministry on the front lines of hunger and homelessness, bringing help, hope, and compassion directly to those in a daily struggle to find food to eat.

Each day, the SoupMobile rolls into a designated parking lot near downtown Dallas with loudspeakers blaring the theme song from *Rocky*. It's the Soup Man's favorite movie and his way of reminding everyone they have the spirit to beat the odds and be the champion of their own life. In addition to providing more than 250,000 meals each year, the SoupMobile also runs a shelter; hosts a Christmas program for five hundred homeless men, women, and children in a downtown hotel; and operates a church for the homeless.

And in case you're wondering, the Soup Man's favorite soup is tomato soup!

- I met **Staff Sergeant Marcus Burleson**, USMC (Ret.), through the Boot Campaign and have been honored to share the public stage with him. Mark knows what it's like to serve, sacrifice, and face overwhelming change and challenge. He served in the marines for more than a decade before he was deployed to Afghanistan, where explosions were a part of his daily life.

A team leader and Explosive Ordnance Disposal technician with the 2nd Platoon, Mark's life was shattered in 2011 while working on dismantling an IED. It exploded in his hands with devastating impact, and the injuries he sustained were extensive: it cost him his hands, seared his face, broke his neck, cracked his jaw, and blinded his left eye. Those injuries required numerous surgeries and two years of recovery at Walter Reed Hospital before he would regain the ability to stand, walk, and speak.

Despite living with chronic pain, Mark continues to serve fellow veterans: helping to provide support for those recovering from their own life-changing injuries and mentoring fellow wounded combat veterans. "It doesn't matter that I've got limitations," Marks says. "It doesn't matter that some of the things I cherished about my previous life aren't there for me anymore. I've still got things to cherish about today and tomorrow."

A West Texas kid who grew up hunting and became a skilled shooter in the Marine Corps, Burleson hadn't held a rifle since the 2011 blast that changed his life. In 2016, he shouldered a custom-made M40A3 designed by C&H Precision Weapons to be fired by a man with no hands. The moment was another impressive step on Mark Burleson's journey to the kind of life he wants for himself and all veterans—limitation and difficulties be damned.

- **SGT. Johnny "Joey" Jones** USMC (Ret.) is another amazing leader I also met through the Boot Campaign. Known to his friends as "Triple J," Jones was raised in Dalton, Georgia and enlisted in the Marine Corps after high school. During his eight years of service, he worked as an Explosive Ordnance Disposal (bomb) Technician, deploying to both Iraq and Afghanistan on three combat tours.

  During his last deployment to Afghanistan, Jones was responsible for disarming and destroying more than 80 improvised explosive devices (IEDs) and thousands of pounds of other unknown bulk explosives. On August 6, 2010; he stepped on and initiated an IED, resulting in the loss of both of his legs above the knee and severe damage to his right forearm and both wrists.

  During two grueling years in recovery at Walter Reed National Military Medical Center in Washington D.C., Joey started a peer visit program which led to an unprecedented year-long fellowship on Capitol Hill with the House Committee on Veterans' Affairs. Joey's contributions there resulted in the creation of an annual fellowship for other inspiring Marine wounded warriors. After his discharge from Walter Reed, Jones enrolled in Georgetown University, earning a bachelor's degree in Liberal Studies. During his time at the university, he was a leader within his student body and co-founded the school's first veteran student organization.

  After losing his childhood best friend to PTSD-related suicide in 2012, Jones decided to make veterans' issues his life's work. He served as a Hero Ambassador and Chief Operating Officer at the Boot Campaign from 2011-2016; and in August 2016 accepted a senior advisor staff position with Zac Brown's Southern Ground to pilot a Warrior Week military transition program.

Today, Joey hosts his own inspirational podcast, "Blown Away with JJJ" and regularly appears as a military analyst and public policy commentator for Fox News.

I've often heard the Original Boot Girls say how much the organization owes **Morgan Luttrell,** US Navy SEAL: (Ret.), who grew up in Texas with his twin brother, Marcus, where they both set their sights on becoming a Navy SEAL. Morgan eventually served 14 years on multiple deployments around the globe and attended Officer Candidate School where he was commissioned as a Naval Special Warfare officer in 2007.

In 2009, Morgan was aboard an army helicopter during a training exercise when it crashed; the force of the explosion resulting in a broken back and severe traumatic brain injury (TBI) that caused multiple cognitive issues for months. After receiving a medical discharge in 2014, Morgan used his own experience to assist veterans suffering from TBI, post-traumatic stress, chronic pain, and addiction in finding effective treatments and medical protocols.

One of the first veteran advocates for the Boot Campaign, Morgan completed a graduate degree in cognitive neuroscience and later served as a Senior Advisor to the Secretary and Director for Translational Research and Applied Analytics in the Department of Energy. Through his work combining the DOE's technology with clinical data from the Department of Veterans Affairs and other agencies, Morgan has become an influential force across several industries. He recently completed his executive education at Harvard Business School focused on professional leadership development and started a company called Stronos Industries, manufacturing eco-friendly signage.

Through it all, Morgan Luttrell has combined his military experience and neuroscience training to focus efforts concerning veterans and their families at the forefront of the national discussion.

- **Ricky Raley** knows something about long roads and journeys. His began in the Indiana Army National Guard where, then Spec. Raley, served as an infantryman in the Guard's Alpha Company, Task Force 1-151—known as the Avengers—as part of Operation Iraqi Freedom. On one combat mission his truck tripped an IED (improvised explosive device). Ricky and two others sustained traumatic brain injuries and were awarded Purple Hearts.

  Raley walked out of Iraq in 2009, but six months after returning home he was involved in a near fatal truck accident leaving him paralyzed from the waist down five months before the birth of his son. Nearly 10 years after that accident, Ricky was introduced to the Boot Campaign and entered its Health and Wellness Program; treatment and training which helps veterans and their families struggling with traumatic brain injury, post-traumatic stress disorder, chronic pain, self-medication, and insomnia.

  The program kick-started his journey to improved mental and physical capability, and inspired Ricky to give back. In August 2018, he hand-cycled 1,500 miles across 14 Days from New York to Florida, raising $150,000 for the Boot Campaign. He returned to the road again in 2019, hand-cycling from the Frontiers of Flight Museum in Dallas to the UDT Navy SEAL Museum in Fort Pierce, Florida; paying it forward again so that more veterans can receive the same individualized treatment he did through the Boot Campaign's Health and Wellness Program.

Building a full-throttle leadership tribe is hard work. Everyone involved needs to connect with a shared vision, accept their individual role, and understand the commitment required to achieve the mission. There is still so much more work to be done in support of our veterans, and as a reminder:

> Fact: Veterans comprise 20 percent of national suicides, with approximately 22 veterans dying by suicide every day.

> Fact: About 10 percent of homeless people are veterans.

> Fact: The unemployment rate for post 9-11 veterans is 9.4 percent.

> Fact: 228,875 veterans served in Iraq or Afghanistan.

> Fact: There are 1.1 million US veterans under age fifty-five living with a disability.

> Fact: I need to be concerned about the welfare of these American heroes, and so do *you*.

Leadership is service, and you don't have to take a thirty-four-day, thirty-four-state, solo motorcycle ride around the United States to learn that. What matters most is that you find a ride that makes a difference; learn everything you can from the people you meet along the way and enjoy every mile because you only get one really good ride in this life.

For everyone who serves, sacrifices, and saddles up, thank you!

# AFTERWORD AND ACKNOWLEDGEMENTS

July 23, 2021

It's been 16 years since the tragic loss of lives in Operation Red Wings, and eight years since I put the kick stand "down" on the Full-Throttle Leadership Ride. A lot happened in the years that followed; political polarization, social unrest, endless conflict, and a Global Pandemic which claimed 500,000 American lives. It's difficult look at our Country today and not ask how did a people so exceedingly generous and genuinely blessed become so dysfunctional, divided, and disconnected?

If only there was a cure for what ails us.

I sincerely believe the same spirit of service, tenacity of goodness and uncompromising compassion I saw first-hand along the Edge of America in 2013 is the only vaccine that can heal our Country. Now, more than ever, I'm reminded of the words Marcus Luttrell penned in his book, Service:

*"Service is selflessness—the opposite of the lifestyle that we see so much of in America today. The things that entertain us do not often lift us up or show us as the people we can rise to become."*

Today, each time I have the opportunity to stand on a stage at a conference or event, I close by inviting veterans and military families to join me for the recognition and applause they so richly deserve. I remind the audience that the answer to *"I'm only one person, what can I do?"* is simple; use your voice.

The Wailin' Jennys, song, "One Voice" has become the soundtrack to those special moments:

*This is the sound of one voice*
*One spirit, one voice*
*The sound of one who makes a choice*
*This is the sound of one voice*

*This is the sound of voices two*
*The sound of me singing with you*
*Helping each other to make it through*
*This is the sound of voices two*

*This is the sound of voices three*
*Singing together in harmony*
*Surrendering to the mystery*
*This is the sound of voices three*

*This is the sound of all of us*
*Singing with love and the will to trust*
*Leave the rest behind it will turn to dust*
*This is the sound of all of us*

*This is the sound of one voice*
*One people, one voice*
*A song for every one of us*
*This is the sound of one voice*

That's leadership; one voice, one heart, one light, one moment in service to others.

The Force Multipliers for Goodness who are working for a Cause and not Applause are the best medicine for America. They lead by example, inspiring all of us to abandon the cultural junk and partisan poison which dominates so much of our lives and instead, find meaningful, sustainable, and powerful ways to give back in the communities where we live, work, and meet.

For everyone who has been part of this wonderful personal and professional "Ride," Thank You.

# ABOUT THE AUTHOR

Steven G. Foster, CMP, is the Managing Partner of Foster+Fathom, a Leadership Training and Goodness Development Group in Dallas, Texas.

An award-winning speaker, consultant, writer, and outspoken advocate for service in the communities where we live, work, and meet; he collaborates with organizations and individuals to build high-performance teams that are "Force Multipliers for the Greater Good."

A Harley-Davidson LIFE member, in 2013 Steven completed a 34-day, 34-state, 13,000-mile solo motorcycle ride along the perimeter of the United States wearing a pair of combat boots to raise awareness and support for the Boot Campaign, a national Veterans Service Organization where he serves as an Ambassador and Advisory Board Member.

Steven and his wife, Wendy, live in Texas, and have two adult children; Aubrey, 23, and Conor, 20. Both Fosters ride motorcycles, were the first husband/wife business team to earn the Certified Meeting Professional (CMP) designation and have been profiled by CNN/Fortune as a small-business success.

CPSIA information can be obtained
at www.ICGtesting.com
Printed in the USA
BVHW050529090622
639249BV00005B/43/J